THE TEN COMMANDMENTS IN MODERN PERSPECTIVE

THE TEN
COMMANDMENTS

□ □ □ □ □ □ □ □ □ □

IN MODERN
PERSPECTIVE

Owen M. Weatherly

□ JOHN KNOX PRESS
Richmond, Virginia

Library of Congress Catalogue Card Number: 61-17440

To
"Mr. Billy"
Who helped a boy become a man

PREFACE

The Ten Commandments outline the basic moral conditions for the realization of the ends for which man exists. These conditions include the giving of one's ultimate devotion only to the Creative Source of all good, the worship of this God alone, personal integrity, acceptance of the rhythmic character of all life, assimilation and transmission of moral values, reverence for life, respect for personality, responsible stewardship, sincerity, and self-control.

The Ten Commandments are all natural laws. Natural laws are the principles by which things are able to realize the ends for which they are created. These principles are built into the nature of things by their Creator as a part of their very being.

Man is unique in being able to understand the laws by which the ends for which he is created may be realized, and in being free to obey them or to disobey them. Because man possesses such understanding and such freedom, he is a "moral" being—that is, a responsible being—and the natural laws which describe the conditions for the fulfillment of his life are called "moral" laws.

Human society can realize the ends for which it was created only to the extent to which it conforms to the requirements of the moral law. The effort toward such a realization must begin with obedience to the Ten Commandments, and whatever is achieved thereafter will survive only so long as it continues to rest on this basic moral foundation. Whenever men lose this foundation, they must find it again before they can begin to rebuild their civilization.

The chief danger to our society consists in its tendency to ignore the moral laws which are the only sure foundation on which its civilization can be built. This book is an effort to recover and restate these fundamental moral laws in their eternal relevance to the ever-changing human situation, in the hope that they may furnish our generation with the necessary impetus for a revitalized struggle toward a closer approximation of the Kingdom of God on earth.

CONTENTS

I

THE PRIORITY
OF GOD

As a means of advertising a series of religious services that were being held in a Highland town, a Scottish newspaper editor employed a most unusual technique. In a notice printed in large letters on the front page the readers of the paper were asked to look on the back page. There, in even larger print, a single question appeared: "Is this where you are putting God?"

This is the question raised in the first of the Ten Commandments. In our thinking and in the ordering of our lives, where shall we put God? Is God merely one among the many values which claim our devotion, or is he the Supreme Good to whom we gladly yield our highest allegiance? Is God a maneuverable commodity we can serve, use, obey, or repudiate at will; or is he the Sovereign Creator of the universe who ever and eternally

> . . . pervades,
> Adjusts, sustains, and agitates the whole?[1]

What place shall God occupy in our lives? Shall we put him on the front page, or on the back page?

THE CONCERN OF THE FIRST COMMANDMENT

The concern of the First Commandment is for the priority of God in human experience. Like the ark, around which the camps of the Israelites were ranged in the wilderness (Numbers 2:1-34),

11

God is to be the center, the hub, the core, the compelling focal point of meaning and power around which every individual life and the whole of human society is to be organized. Just as the cloud went before the liberated tribes of Israel on their way to Canaan, as the trusted and trustworthy guide in all their journeyings and determiner of the time and place of their encampment (Numbers 9:15-23), so God is to be in the forefront of every human movement as the one by whose will every attitude and activity of our lives is to be ordered.

The First Commandment does not raise the question of God's existence. It simply lays down a rule regarding God's rank in terms of human loyalty. The existence of God is not argued; it is assumed. In the religious tradition in which we find the Ten Commandments, there is no place for argument about the existence of God. To the Hebrews, God was not a premise to be proved, but a Personality to be experienced. He was not a conclusion to be reached at the end of a series of logical deductions, but the ultimate, concrete starting point of all their thinking. In the experience of this people, the evidence for the existence of God was too deep for doubt and too personal for proof.

We shall follow in this discussion the example of those to whom the Decalogue was first delivered. Like them, we believe that "in the beginning" was God, and that apart from him there is no starting point from which we can move with any hope of arriving at anything that is worth the time and effort it would take to get there. I believe that God exists and that he is the kind of Being who might reasonably give such a Commandment as the one we are considering and expect it to be obeyed. I do not believe that there are any means whatever by which I can prove the existence of such a God to anyone else. The best I can do in the effort to improve another person's attitude toward the existence of God is to help guide him into those experiences of life in which he can have and become consciously aware of his own personal encounter with God.

Man's effort to prove the existence of God is forever futile because the reality of God impinges upon his perceptive awareness in such a direct and immediate way and at such a fundamental level of his own being that no unassailable evidence of the encounter can be submitted to another person. We can have the certainty of the existence of God for ourselves, but not the satisfaction of proving that existence to anyone else.

The effort to prove the existence of God is frustrated not only by our own inability to submit adequate evidence of the fact but also by the other person's inability or unreadiness to receive it as such. What constitutes convincing evidence of the existence of God for me may not be acceptable or convincing to another person.

This is the sense in which faith—man's experience of God and his commitment of himself to God—is always the gift of God himself. The Messiah comes only to those whom God makes ready for his coming. In terms of his own capacities man can seek for God, but he cannot find him. We encounter God, but only because in our seeking God finds us.

Proving the existence of God, even if it were possible, would serve no useful purpose. No one I know needs such proof. Certainly those who believe in the existence of God do not need it. And I do not know of anyone who does not believe in the existence of God. All the so-called "atheists" I know are not denying the existence of God. What they are denying is the existence of their own caricature of God, in whose existence nobody believes.

But even if everyone were convinced of the existence of God, such universal belief would not necessarily serve any useful purpose. It is a small thing to believe in the existence of God. The devils believe and tremble at the implications of such a reality. But belief and trembling are not enough. In his relation to God, man's problem is not disbelief, but disobedience. In assuming the existence of God and in centering its attention on man's response to God, the First Commandment comes to grips with the human problem at its most crucial point.

Another entanglement the First Commandment wisely and skillfully avoids is the foolish and futile assertion that there is but one god. This does not mean that the First Commandment permits a polytheistic scattering of man's ultimate allegiance.

That is precisely what it prohibits. The First Commandment demands that man's ultimate allegiance be given to God alone; but it does not deny or overlook the fact that there are lesser things than God to which man can and frequently does give himself in the ultimate sense in which he may rightfully give himself only to God. This is to say that the First Commandment understands and acknowledges the existence and nature of the gods, an understanding and recognition which we are the poorer for having lost. It understands and acknowledges the fact that anything, however worthy or unworthy, to which a man gives his ultimate devotion and service is his god.

The religious genius of the Hebrew people was never given to the task of personalizing and naming and mythologizing the vast number of gods who compete for the ultimate devotion of human lives, as other ancient people did. They were prevented from doing this by the appearance among them at a very early period of a persistent monotheistic faith in the one God who alone is worthy of man's ultimate devotion. There were serious defections from this faith among them, but it remained strong enough to keep them from any prolonged acknowledgment of any object worthy of man's ultimate devotion except God.

When man gives his ultimate devotion to anything other than God and makes it the ruling principle in his life, that thing becomes his god, and—with reference to his own attitude toward it—he puts that thing "before God," or in the place of God. This is the practice which is prohibited in the First Commandment: the practice of making anything other than God the ultimate principle by which our lives are shaped and ordered.

THE GODS WHO COMPETE

While the galaxy of personalized gods familiar to ancient man did not figure systematically or prominently in the mythology or the liturgy of the Hebrews, they became well acquainted with many of these deities through their contacts with other cultures. These people tarried long in the land of Egypt where there were as many local gods as there were hamlets. They lived there in close touch with people who worshipped Ra, Ptah, Osiris, Isis, and Horus. In polytheistic Canaan they rubbed elbows with Baal, Asherah, Molech, and Dagon. Frequently large numbers of these Israelites joined their Gentile neighbors in the worship of some one or more of these pagan gods. The hard core of Hebrews monotheists remained consistently true to their faith in one God; but even these were constantly reminded by the impressive array of pagan deities which surrounded them that there were things other than God to which men could and frequently did give their supreme allegiance, and that those things to which men give their ultimate devotion are their gods in every sense of the word.

The personification and deification of the things to which men give their ultimate devotion were carried to a point of almost unbelievable refinement in the cultures of both Greece and Rome. Among these peoples practically every object of man's ultimate devotion was personified, named, and given his own peculiar place in the complex hierarchy of cultural dieties. While this deification of the things to which men give their supreme allegiance was carried to the extreme in the ancient world of the Greeks and Romans, and was therefore finally frowned upon by the best thinkers among them, the personification of the objects of man's ultimate devotion had its good points. For one thing, it kept men ever aware of the vast number of things which were constantly competing for their supreme allegiance, and ever aware of the fact that the thing to which a man gives his absolute allegiance is in reality his god. Furthermore, this deifying of the object of man's ultimate devotion enabled him to identify the various competitors for his supreme allegiance, and thus gave him the advantage of being able to recognize these claimants to his loyalty for what they really are.

In departing from the ancient practice of personifying and deifying the things which compete for his loyalty, modern man has not eliminated the gods; he has only eliminated his advantage in dealing with them. All the ancient deities are still with us. Old gods never die; they merely change their dress and adopt im-

proved techniques of deception and allurement. Now as in the
days of Oedipus

"Gods meet gods, and justle in the dark."[2]

The only difference is that we do not now recognize them for
what they are. We do not recognize them as gods competing or
conspiring to win our absolute loyalty.

The ancient Greeks were in a better position than we are in
the continuing struggle with these persistent deities, because they
had the whole lot of them carefully catalogued. They had their
names, addresses, profiles, and fingerprints all neatly filed and
available for ready reference. This was valuable information. A
man ought to be able to identify his gods. For man's choice is
never between the true God and no god, but between the true
God and some lesser object which claims his ultimate devotion
and thus becomes his god.

In the social register of ancient deities, there was a group of
prominent feminine divinities whom the Greeks called the
Moirai, the goddesses of Fate. These subtle sisters are still very
much alive. They appear at every important social function in
America. Theirs are the sweet voices that tell us there is no use
getting upset over poverty, injustice, waste, immorality, incom-
petence, or the danger of war. All these things are determined,
they would have us believe, by powers that are too complex
and too great for us to even understand, let alone successfully
oppose. The best thing to do, they insist, is to accept things as
they are and be thankful that we happen to be educated, socially
acceptable, and economically secure ourselves and therefore im-
mune to many of life's more troublesome irritations.

We do not call these goddesses of Fate the Moirai any more.
Their modern name is "They." "They" start all the vicious
rumors. "They" believe and say that a whole people is inferior
because of a certain pigmentation of the skin; therefore, it has
to be true and I must protect myself from them. Don't go to the
polls on Tuesday because "They" have already decided the issues
in private political caucuses, and your vote won't accomplish

anything anyway. Don't bother to speak out against war because "They" won't pay any attention to one small voice. Don't work for social justice because "They" have all the power, and "They" are going to keep things as they are now.

Discussing the company's color discrimination in its lunch counter service, the president of a large chain store explained to stockholders that the firm's policy on serving Negroes in certain of its outlets was governed completely by local customs. "These are customs we can't change," he said, adding "as attitudes and customs change our practice will change promptly."[3] Who made these customs? This executive doesn't bother to raise the question, but the answer is obvious. "They" did. Who alone is credited with having the power to change these sacred customs in order to make it possible for the owners and managers of the company to bring their business policies and practices into conformity with the moral principles by which they profess to live? "They" do.

We never build an altar to the goddesses of Fate today. We are much too sophisticated to acknowledge the existence of the Moirai. But everyday we bow before the mystic, invisible, life-determining force we call "They." At every point of testing we yield to what we imagine to be the determinative, inexorable opinion and will of the dominant forces in our culture. We accept the most popular ideas as the will of the gods. We capitulate to the wishes of the most aggressive elements in our culture as to the hand of Fate itself. We have no faith in any ability to shape our own destiny. We yield to the determination of whatever forces of custom, or "respectability," or fear, or intimidation, or reprisal that may be brought to bear upon us. In our preferences, in our decisions, and in the giving of our ultimate loyalty and service, the modern, daring, ever-present, deterministic god "They" is constantly being put "before" the eternal "I Am" of the Decalogue.

Prominent also in the modern pantheon of deities is the god Self. When Greece ruled the world this god was called Narcissus, and he was known to have acquired the particular traits of character by which he is distinguished among the gods as a result of having fallen in love with his own reflection in a pool. The full name by which he prefers to be addressed in polite society today is Enlightened Self Interest. But no matter by what name he is known, or in what century or civilization he is served, he has one rule of faith and practice which he imposes on all his devotees: *Self is the measure, the end, and the object of all existence.* From this single, fundamental maxim stem all the questions—the answers to which determine all the attitudes, decisions, and actions of all the followers of the god Self: "What's in it for me?" "Does it pay off in cash?" "Will it get votes?" "Does it provide maximum security for my family?" "Will it sell soap?" "Is there room for me at the top?" "Will it keep the party in power?" "How will it affect the real estate value of my home?" "Is this going to affect my popularity with the 'best' people?"

Widespread devotion to the god Self threatens the very existence of our civilization. Homes break up because husbands are too much occupied with the puffed-up image of their own importance to take time to understand their wives. Families disintegrate because wives put their own social ambitions before husband and children, and even before God. Disastrous foreign policies are shaped to serve the selfish interests of those who control the powers of government. "Justice" in the courts is interpreted in terms of protecting the social and political and economic advantages of the dominant group in the community. Large sections of the country's economy are planned and operated for immediate personal gain without regard for the permanent well-being of all the people.

It is in the service of the god Self that we become bigots, dogmatists, demagogues, and dictators, obsessed with the imagined superiority of our own ideas and intolerant of the opinions of other people. *Our* race, *our* color, *our* religion, *our* culture, *our* form of government, and *our* economic system become the only ones about which there can be any possible good, and all others degenerate into something totally inferior, something to be feared and opposed and destroyed with unreasoning rage and violence. The service of the god Self separates us from the good which might act redemptively in our lives. It blinds us to reality and deprives us of any ground on which we can stand to view ourselves objectively.

Every god of classic myth and ancient shrine has his corps of faithful followers in modern America. The pleasure-loving deity whom the Romans called Bacchus, the god of wine, reveling, and drunkenness, has a temple on practically every street corner in the land. More people take the cup at his table than at the table of our Lord Christ. Five million living Americans have been sacrificed on his altars, and this pitiful horde of helpless alcoholics is being constantly augmented at the rate of fifteen hundred every day.

Eros, the god of physical attraction and sensual indulgence, is served with slavish devotion and fanatic fervor on an almost universal scale. Devotion to Plutus, the divine personification of material values, is by no means confined to those countries which openly follow a philosophy of materialism. His followers, those who put material values above moral and spiritual values, are equally numerous in America. The service of Vesta, goddess of the hearth, the city, and state, is abundantly evident in the devotion of millions to a narrow provincialism, and in the dedication of millions more to an outmoded and suicidal form of absolute nationalism.

As these illustrations clearly indicate, some of the things to which man gives his ultimate devotion are evil in themselves. Others are not evil; they are simply not God. But the First Commandment is violated in one case no less than in the other. For the First Commandment forbids the giving of one's ultimate devotion to anything whatever other than God, no matter how good it may be in itself. It is in this respect that many "good" people disobey the First Commandment and threaten themselves with destruction. One distraught husband, agonizing over the pathetic debacle of a broken home, realized too late how easy it is to give to some lesser good the devotion that belongs only to the Supreme Good. Explaining the failure of his marriage, he said: "For twenty years, I made my work my god." There is nothing wrong with work as such. But to give it the devotion that belongs only to God is to invite certain disaster.

To serve as God any one of the lesser things we have mentioned is a misdirection of devotion which would seem to be the most unwise course that man is ever likely to follow. What many of us frequently attempt, however, is even more foolish. We compound futility with frustration by trying to serve *all* of them. As Christians we profess to serve only God, the Father of our Lord Jesus Christ. But what too often happens in actual practice is that we share the service we owe to him with many other gods, or run with our whole devotion to first one and then the other. No man can serve two masters, but every man can try, and most of us do. And whenever the attempt is made it always results in the disintegration of personality and the loss of moral integrity. Psychiatrists call this erratic and irresponsible scattering of our loyalties and our service schizophrenia. Theologians call it polytheism. By any name it spells disaster for human personality and for human society.

The God Who Commands

A man's god is the thing to which he gives his supreme devotion, the thing he puts before everything else, the thing which he accepts as the ruling principle in his life and to which he makes every thought and action conform. This ultimate devotion can be *given* to anything. But only one Reality is *worthy* of such devotion. This is the basic difference between worshiping the gods and God. The difference consists not primarily in the kind of loyalty man gives but in the worthiness of the object to which he gives it. The kind of loyalty a man is able to give to anything is determined ultimately, of course, by the character of the object to which it is given. This is why man's attempt to give his ultimate allegiance to anything other than God always tends to become a frantic and self-destructive attempt to give his absolute devotion to many things. Since nothing other than God is ever able to satisfy man's inherent need for an absolute principle to live by, his attempt to find such a principle in anything other than God becomes a desperate running with his allegiance to first one object of devotion and then another, or an even more disconcerting effort to serve several at once.

This is the futile, self-destructive practice which is prohibited in the First Commandment. But no matter how well we may understand the danger and futility of giving our supreme devotion to things not worthy of it, we shall continue to do it until we can be led to an appreciative awareness and sincere acceptance of the one reality which *is* worthy of our ultimate loyalty. We are never persuaded to transfer our ultimate devotion from the objects which are unworthy of it to the one object which is worthy of it except by the authoritative and compulsive power of that worthy object itself. Just as we are weakened and may be destroyed by the inferiorities and inadequacies of the objects of our ultimate devotion when we erroneously give such devotion to objects which are not worthy of it, we are and must be sustained in the giving of our supreme loyalty to the one object which is worthy of it by the absolute power and goodness of that object itself.

What *is* worthy of our ultimate loyalty? What is worthy of being the absolute principle to which our every thought and action may be made to conform? What is good enough to sustain and magnify the good that is in us and overcome the evil that constantly threatens to destroy us? What is wise enough and powerful enough to lead us into the realization of those ends for which we were created? On such an object man might be persuaded to center consistently all the loyalty and service and devotion which he is prone to scatter among the gods if he were able to find it and identify it. What does the First Commandment say with regard to the identity of this object of man's supreme devotion before whom no other gods are to be put?

The First Commandment itself says nothing explicit about the identity of the object for whom man's supreme allegiance is claimed. The First Commandment is set in a context in which the Object for whom man's ultimate devotion is claimed is himself the speaker. Thus the one for whom the Commandment claims the first place in man's allegiance and the one who gives the Commandment are the same. It could not be otherwise. The kind of devotion demanded in the First Commandment is of such a nature that it can be demanded only by him for whom it is demanded. By him and for him who issues it, the First Commandment demands the first place in man's life. Such a demand can be made only by one whose authority and goodness are supreme and absolute. By definition there can be only one such Being.

In the prologue to the Ten Commandments the one who issues the Commandments, including this one demanding for himself the first place in man's devotion, identifies himself to the Hebrews as "the LORD your God, who brought you out of the land of Egypt, out of the house of bondage" (Exodus 20:2). This identification was sufficient for those to whom the Commandment was first given. They knew this One who had brought them out of Egypt. They knew him as the eternal Creator of all that exists. They knew him as the One who sustains and orders the universe. They knew him as One of absolute authority and absolute goodness. They knew him as the ground of all being and as the Person who enters into human experience and makes himself known to man. They knew him as Provider, Protector, Lawgiver, and Judge. They knew him as One who puts upon man the stamp of his own image and takes positive action to redeem him when by the misuse or disuse of his freedom he threatens to destroy himself.

Apart from the existence of such a God the First Commandment is inconceivable. It could not be given, understood, or obeyed. The First Commandment was meaningful to the Hebrews to whom it was first given because such a God does exist and because they had experienced him as a concrete, creative, redemptive, and sustaining force in their lives. This is the God who is manifested and magnified in the earthly life and eternally living Person of Jesus Christ. This is the God who enters human experience and impinges upon human consciousness today as he did in the days when the Ten Commandments were given. We sometimes use more technical and less personal terms when we try to describe God today, but the reality we experience, the reality which makes the First Commandment meaningful and our obedience to it possible, is the same sovereign Being who brought the children of Israel out of Egyptian bondage and continues to act redemptively in history. He is the Father of our Lord Jesus Christ. He is absolute, eternal, creative good. As the ultimate good, he is ultimate love, and ultimately redemptive. As the single absolute and all-sufficient Reality by which all life and being are understood and ordered, he is absolutely and eternally sovereign. He is that source and force of good in life which works creatively toward the increase of meaning and value in human experience. Without impairing human freedom, he is able to redeem man from the destruction which he tends to bring upon himself. Without eliminating the possibility of evil, he is able to prevail against it and to continue the increase of good. This is the God who gave the First Commandment. He alone has the authority to give such a Commandment because he alone has the power to transform man into the kind of creature who can and will obey it.

THE MAN WHO OBEYS

The man who obeys the First Commandment must understand the nature of the gods and the nature of God. The First Commandment is intended to settle the most basic question in every human life, namely: What will be my first concern? What will be the thing to which I will give my first and supreme loyalty? What will I love and serve above all else? What will be the principle by which I will interpret and evaluate every other thing and by which I will order every aspect of my life? The choice is between God and any one or all of the gods. This means that the choice is not merely or even mainly between absolute good and absolute evil. More often the choice is between the absolute good and some limited good, between the "creative good" and some "created good," between the ground of all being and some aspect of being, between absolute truth and some approximation of the truth. The gods are not all totally bad. Some of them are good. But none of them is God.

For the man who would obey the First Commandment an understanding of the nature of God and the gods is essential but not sufficient. The end of the First Commandment is obedience to God's will as he is given the first place in man's devotion, loyalty, and service. Understanding of what God is and what the gods are is only a means to this end, not the end itself. Intellectual acceptance of the fact that God is the absolute Good who alone is worthy of man's ultimate devotion amounts to nothing apart from the commitment of one's life to the will of God. This is the truth which Jesus emphasized repeatedly in the Sermon on the Mount. Many of Jesus' contemporaries saw in his life and teaching a manifestation of the Person and will of God. They understood this fact with their minds and confessed it with their lips. But intellectual assent and verbal affirmation were not enough. To those who went this far but no farther Jesus said: "Not every one who says to me, 'Lord, Lord,' shall enter the kingdom of heaven, but he who does the will of my Father who is in heaven" (Matthew 7:21). He pointed to the Gentiles who gave their ultimate devotion to the gods of material value and said to his disciples: "But seek first his kingdom and his righteousness, and all these things shall be yours as well" (Matthew 6:33) .

The First Commandment does not deny that beside God there are other good things which may make a proper claim on man's attention. It does not deny to man any one of these good things. What the First Commandment does is make clear the distinction between good things and the Source of all good things. It also makes clear the difference which should exist between man's response to good things and his response to the Source of all good things. All good belongs to man—for his enjoyment and for the enrichment of his life. To the Source of all good, man himself belongs. To a limited, created good, man may properly give a limited devotion. Man's ultimate devotion may be given only to the creative Source of all good.

II

THE WORSHIP
OF GOD

The concern of the Second Commandment is for the true worship of God. It deals with the danger of allowing the means of worship to usurp the place which belongs only to the object of worship.

The purpose of the Second Commandment is not to impoverish the experience of worship by a limitation on the means of worship. Its aim is to safeguard the purity of worship by limiting the object of worship to God alone.

WHAT THE SECOND COMMANDMENT PROHIBITS

The initial announcement of the Second Commandment seems to imply a prohibition against the use of certain objects even as aids to worship. Indeed, taken by itself, this first pronouncement appears to proscribe the creation of any tangible representation of any object for any purpose whatever. "You shall not make yourself a graven image, or any likeness of anything that is in heaven above, or that is in the earth beneath, or that is in the water under the earth" (Exodus 20:4). If this were indeed a decree against the making of any representation of any aspect of reality for any purpose, it would rule out the arts of painting and sculpture, and perhaps even some forms of music and literature, along with the making of images for use as means or objects of worship. Such an extremely radical interpretation of this part of the Second Commandment fortunately has never been held for

long by any significant segment of society. The statement immediately following the one just quoted, "you shall not bow down
to them or serve them" (Exodus 20:5) makes it unmistakably
clear that the concern of the Second Commandment for image-
making is limited altogether to the use of images in man's
experience of worship.

As an item of moral legislation of a universal character the
prohibition of the Second Commandment applies only to the use
of images as objects of worship. It does not condemn the production of representations of any aspect of reality as work of art.
It does not categorically prohibit the use of such representations
as aids to the worship of God. It is true that at particular points
in the history of both Hebrew and Christian experience this Commandment has been interpreted as a prohibition against the use
of images even as aids to worship, and strenuous attempts have
been made to enforce it as such. There is some reason to believe
that there were periods in primitive times when the injunction
against even the *making* of certain types of images was interpreted
literally, and that attempts were made to enforce it literally. The
wording of the first part of the Second Commandment lends some
credence to the supposition that this was the case in Israel at the
time the Decalogue was given to the Hebrews.

The total import of the Second Commandment as a whole,
however, as well as the legal and cultural context in which this
injunction is found, does not indicate that anything more was
intended in the giving of this law as an item of universal moral
legislation than the prohibition of images as objects of worship.
In a companion piece of legislation the same God who gave the
Decalogue to the Hebrews also gave them specific commandments
calling for the furnishing of the tabernacle with tangible representations of various aspects of reality. They were commanded to
"make two cherubim of gold" to rest on the two ends of the mercy
seat which was to be placed on top of the ark of the covenant.
The bowls on the candelabra to be used in the tabernacle worship
were to be shaped like almonds and adorned with engravings
of flowers. With what appears to have been divine approval, the
Jerusalem temple constructed by Solomon was adorned with

graven images of flowers, palm trees, pomegranates, lions, oxen, and cherubim.

Unmistakably, the universal intent of the Second Commandment is to prohibit the use of images as objects of worship. Insofar as the making of images or likenesses of any aspect of reality is prohibited, it is quite clear that the prohibition is against the making of such images and other representations of reality *to be used as objects of worship*.

THE NECESSITY AND PERIL OF SYMBOLISM

The danger against which the prohibition of the Second Commandment guards is one which is ever and inevitably present in man's necessary use of symbols to represent reality. Man has a direct, immediate experience of reality. This immediate contact with reality is both sensory and extrasensory. It is facilitated both by what we call the "physical" senses, and by spiritual or intuitive prehensions. To speak of "extrasensory"—or, more properly, "extraphysical"—contacts is not to introduce a "supernatural" element into man's experience of reality. It is simply to recognize that man is a spiritual as well as a physical being, and that the spiritual is as sensitive to other realities as the physical, if, indeed, not more so. Whether collected sensorily or "extrasensorily"—by physical contact or spiritual encounter—the data of immediate experience is and must be conceptualized and interpreted intellectually before it becomes what we can call knowledge, and before it has any meaning even for the one who has had the experience. This is to say that the data, or content, of any and every sort of experience always enters conscious awareness as some kind of mental image. We encounter reality in moments of direct, immediate experience, but the varied contents of these moments of experience are sorted out and put into meaningful relationship by a process of conceptualization, rational interpretation, and organization which produces an intelligible pattern of mental images.

Clearly, then, in every effort to understand and interpret reality—that is, in every effort to collect and communicate knowledge—man is forced to use symbols to represent realities. The vision of a rose in bloom is a mental image constructed out of the data collected by the sensory organs of sight and organized and interpreted by the mind. An idea is a mental image, derived by means of an intellectual organization and interpretation of certain data received in an empirical encounter with some aspect of reality. Language is altogether a matter of symbolic representation of real things. Words are merely symbols of the realities they represent. Words are actually small mental images to which phonetic or graphic expression is given. To define a word is to bring into focus the particular mental image which has been formed as a result of man's experience of and his attempt to identify the reality which the word represents.

Our aim is not to explore all of the interesting facets of either epistemology or semantics, but simply to call attention to the necessary use of symbols in all human experience, and to point out the peril which is always present in the use of such representations of reality. It is the inevitable peril of confusion and perversion. For a symbol to be meaningful and useful it is necessary that there be a close association in our thinking between the symbol and the thing it represents. The peril lies in the tendency of this necessary association to become absolute identification. When the distinction between the symbol and the reality represented by it is obscured, we become confused and frequently give to the symbol itself the devotion and service of which only the reality it represents is worthy. In this preoccupation with the symbol as such, we tend to lose sight altogether of the reality represented. The symbol which was intended to be a mere means to an end— namely, a more proper relating of ourselves to the reality represented by the symbol—is perverted and becomes an end in itself. Words, for example, are frequently indentified with, then substituted for, the good deeds they are designed to describe and represent. This was the fault on the part of certain Christians in the early church which caused the author of James to ask: "If a brother or sister is ill-clad and in lack of daily food, and one of you says to them, 'Go in peace, be warmed and filled,' without giving them the things needed for the body, what does it profit?"

(James 2:15-16.) This is the practice which has come to be known as "lip-service," and against which the author of I John warned the early church when he said: "let us not love in word or speech but in deed and in truth" (I John 3:18).

In the ultimate analysis the problem posed in the Second Commandment is the problem of appearance and reality. We experience real things concretely and immediately, but we never experience the whole of anything, and the whole of what we do experience is never presented perfectly in conscious awareness. We experience reality, but what enters our consciousness is the appearance of reality. This appearance of reality is what the mind makes out of the data derived from experience.

It is with reference to appearance that the question of truth arises. Reality simply is. Appearance is true or false, depending upon the closeness with which it conforms to the reality it represents or reflects.

For various reasons, appearance in human experience never conforms perfectly to reality. For one thing man is not equipped to comprehend reality in its wholeness. Appearances are mental images, and mental images are mere symbols of reality. All symbols are simplifications of reality. A mental image is a manageable symbol of an unimaginable reality. Appearance fails to conform perfectly to reality also because of the fallibility and perverseness of the human mind. We deceive ourselves unavoidably and others deliberately. For these reasons, among others, human truth is never *the* truth. The temptation to make *our* truth *the* truth—to absolutize the particular appearance of reality which is produced by the image-making activity of our own minds—is a part of the grave danger involved in man's use of symbols.

While, as we have seen, the use of symbols poses a problem in all human experience, it is particularly dangerous in man's worship of God. This is true because of the spiritual, intangible nature of God's being, which necessitates a greater reliance upon symbols in our dealings with him, particularly in our acts of devotion. It is true also because of the unparalleled dimensions of his being. The great disparity between the fullness of his being and our capacity to comprehend it increases our dependence upon symbols and decreases the accuracy of our image-making.

IMAGE-MAKING IN MODERN WORSHIP

While almost everyone will concede the accuracy of this general analysis of image-making and our tendency to misuse symbols, few people seem to be able to recognize the problem as it appears in Christian worship today. Most of us are inclined to agree with the popular opinion that "the worship of various gods and the use of idols is no longer one of our dangers."[1] One contemporary thinker dismisses the subject with the observation that idolatry is "a practice in which we have not been tempted to engage for more than two thousand years."[2] Such views are not substantiated either by the facts of church history or the facts of contemporary religious experience.

In large segments of the Christian church image-worship of one form or another has been practiced with only brief interruptions from at least as far back as the fifth century. It has been the cause of some of the most serious controversies in the history of the Christian church. By the eighth century the practice had become so common and so crass that Emperor Leo III issued an edict in 725-726 prohibiting the use of images in the Byzantine Empire. This ban on image-worship aroused strong opposition on the part of the most powerful ecclesiastics of the time. It was strenuously opposed by both Germanus, the Patriarch of Constantinople, and Gregory II, the Pope of Rome. Continuing the policies of Leo III, Emperor Constantine V called a Council of the church to meet in 753-754 in the palace of Hieria on the Asiatic shore of the Bosporus to deal with the problem. A decree of this Council definitely and strongly condemned image-worship. The issue, however, was far from settled. During the minority of Constantine VI, the rule of the Empire was entrusted to his mother, Irene, who was determined to restore image-worship. In 787, in the Bithynian city of Nicaea, she convened the seventh and last Ecumenical Council in the history of the Eastern Church. By decree of this council image-worship was restored.[3] Image-worship was challenged again in connection with the Reformation movement in the sixteenth century. While formal image-worship has been banned in practically all Protestant churches, the Reformation did not seriously affect the practice in the Roman and Eastern Churches.

It is plausibly argued by those who favor the use of images that they are aids to worship and not objects of worship, and that therefore the practice does not violate the Second Commandment. It cannot be denied that images are legitimate aids to worship and that there is nothing in the Second Commandment which prohibits their use as such. A question arises, however, in worship as in other experiences, as to when an image of any kind ceases to be an instrument which serves us and becomes a master who controls us. This happens in worship when the means by which we express our devotion to God becomes the object of our devotion. When this happens, the Second Commandment is violated, no matter what the original intent may have been regarding the use of the symbol involved.

While our record as Protestants with regard to the formal use of tangible images in worship may be less clouded than that of some other religious groups, the assumption that image-worship is less common or less disastrous among us than among others is open to serious question. It is true that we make little if any use of the traditional images commonly employed in the worship of other branches of the Christian church. But there are less obvious images which capture our devotion in more subtle ways than a copper crucifix or a marble statue.

An aid to worship becomes an object of worship, hence in every sense of the word an idol, when we give to it more attention and real devotion than we give to God himself. The number of such things which enter religious experience as aids to worship and end up as objects of worship are legion. A particular aid to worship which has become the object of our worship can usually be identified by the fuss we make over it. When the substitution of commercial wafers for the sliced bread always used in the communion service at "Old First Church" sends certain members of the congregation into hysterical tirades of protest, it is not difficult to see what it is they have been worshiping. When those who support every effort in "evangelism" and "foreign missions" with pious enthusiasm and never miss an opportunity to proclaim with open pride their "love for all mankind" react with violent opposition to the slightest suggestion that people with skin of a different color be allowed to hold membership in "their" church, it may be reasonably assumed that what they are worshiping is not God but their own idea of what constitutes a desirable "religious" fellowship. A change in the order of service, however clearly beneficial to the sincere worship of God, will frequently send even the most "liberal" members of the congregation into tantrums of childish rebellion. Custom is seldom fashioned into a bronze image or a granite statue, but as a mental habit or emotional fixation it can be equally rigid, equally useless, and equally pernicious as a diversion from the worship of God.

All too many of us who go to church to worship God end up bowing semi-consciously before nothing more meaningful than habit or tradition. As late as the mid-nineteenth century it was noticed that the members of a Danish Protestant church observed what was in that setting a very strange custom of bowing when they came to a certain spot on the wall. There was nothing different about this part of the wall, and when questions were asked, no member of the congregation could shed any light on the origin or meaning of the custom. Their fathers had done this, so they did it, although no one then living knew why. The reason for this practice was revealed when the walls were cleaned and underneath a layer of whitewash there was found at this spot on the wall a Roman Catholic Madonna. For years, without knowing and apparently without caring why, these Protestant worshipers had been bowing before the place where the Madonna was once visible and, to their Roman Catholic forefathers, meaningful. What many of us are worshiping in our own churches today is not the living God but some custom or tradition, the origin or significance of which we no longer understand. In many cases what Jesus said to the first-century Samaritans can be said with equal justification to twentieth-century Christians: "You worship what you do not know" (John 4:22).

theological conceits today are to be found among the "funda-
talists." They can be found also in distressingly large num-
among those who like to call themselves "liberals."

nstances of image-worship are nowhere more common than
connection with the innumerable "memorials" which crowd
ir Christian worship. There is a legitimate place in our Christian
xperience for recognizing and expressing love and appreciation
or our fellowmen. The practice Paul recommended to the Roman
Christians when he suggested that they "outdo one another in
showing honor" (Romans 12:10) is a good one to follow in
Christian fellowship, but it should never be confused with our
worship of God. It is extremely difficult to keep our worship directed exclusively to God when the sanctuary, pews, hymnbooks,
pulpit, Bible, organ, and every other tangible and tagable commodity we use as an aid to worship is ostentatiously labeled as a
memorial gift in honor of the donor himself or someone else to
whom he wishes to set up an imperishable monument. There is
nearly always in the giving of such memorials and their injection
into our services of worship some intention that they be used to
the glory of God, but the strength of the connection which these
gifts have with certain human beings and the honor which is
claimed in perpetuity for these human beneficiaries tend to out-
weigh the honor which they direct toward God. These memorials
are usually very petty in terms of their intrinsic worth—frequently
being of little more value than the conspicuous plaque which
must inevitably be displayed along with them—but the devotion
which they are able to claim for themselves is tremendous. It is a
matter of record in many churches that more burning indignation
can be aroused in the congregation by failing to insert in the order
of service the proper acknowledgment of the memorial flowers
provided for the pulpit than by the most spirited sermon on the
social injustices that plague the community. Our insistence upon
the injection of these memorials to ourselves and to other human
beings into our worship of God, and the frequency with which
they cease to be aids to worship and become objects of worship,
confirm the fact that the image to which man's ultimate devotion

Another familiar group of images c
modern churches are the theological dog
ground. Theological concepts are necessa
useful aids to worship. Intellectual concepts,
aids to worship, frequently usurp the place
claiming for themselves the devotion they are
us give to God. A theological concept, like any c
a mental image—an intellectual symbol—of sc
reality. Specifically, a theological concept is an intell
of some truth about God, or about man's relationship
the truth about any aspect of the reality of God *as we*
what that reality *appears to us to be.* The truth about
our relationship to him contained in our theological con
never and can never be the absolute truth. We have divine
tions of truth, of course, but even this divinely revealed tru
for each of us only what *we* understand it to be. Even as imper.
embodiments of truth—that is, as imperfect symbols of reality.
our theological concepts can be helpful aids to our worship o
God. It is only when we absolutize our theological concepts that
they divert our devotion from God to themselves and thus usurp
the place of God in our worship.

Whether a person is worshiping the true God or his own crys-
talized concept of some aspect of the reality of God can usually
be judged with considerable accuracy by the degree of tolerance
or intolerance with which he reacts to those whose theological
concepts differ from his own. If he reacts with uncompromising
hostility to all opposing views, and with a frantic defense of his
own, and a refusal to fellowship and co-operate with those who
differ with him, he is most likely worshiping his own theological
concepts and not God, for God needs no such fanatical defense,
and does not inspire such behavior on the part of those who worship him. Too many of those who worship in the name of Christ
today are giving more of their real devotion to the defense and
propagation of their own theological concepts than to the God
whose Son they profess to serve. It is significant also that, contrary
to what was once mainly true and to what is still generally felt to
be true, not all of those who are worshiping the image of their

is most likely to be diverted is his own inflated opinion of
himself.

LAW AND THE GOD ABOVE LAW

The injunction against the making of images to be used as
objects of worship is accompanied in the Second Commandment
by a pronouncement of the universal law of cause and effect and
the certainty of the everlasting mercy of God. The law of cause
and effect—what I have called in another context "The Law of
the Harvest"[4]—is familiar to scientists and theologians alike as a
dependable axiom in the realms of both physics and morals. In the
area of moral experience we describe the working of this law by
saying that every action has its own peculiar consequences. "For
whatever a man sows, that he will also reap" (Galatians 6:7) is the
way Paul expressed it. When the author of the Second Commandment represented God as saying, "I the LORD your God am
a jealous God, visiting the iniquity of the fathers upon the
children to the third and the fourth generation of those who
hate me," he was simply affirming this law. This ascription to
God of the attitude of jealousy—an emotion which we commonly think of as being an unmitigated evil—has seriously de-
creased the prestige and effectiveness of the Second Commandment in modern culture. This is evident not in any open rebellion against the injunction but in the fact that, being unable
to understand this ascription of jealousy to God, modern worshipers ignore it, and along with it, the rest of the Commandment
also.

The word "jealousy" is nearly always used now to describe an
attitude of inordinate possessiveness which shows itself in hateful
resentment against others, an emotion which we cannot possibly
reconcile with the concept of the character of God contained in
the Christian faith. It would help the situation immensely if we
could realize that while the word is generally used in this bad
sense, it has a better side. Although the word is not commonly
used in this sense now, it can mean serious concern for the
honor of that which is highly esteemed. Thus, to say that

a statesman is jealous of some country other than his own usually means that he envies, suspects, fears, and hates that nation; but when a patriot says that he is "jealous" of his own country, he may be properly using the word to express the fact that he feels a deep concern for the honor of his native land. This is the sense in which Elijah used the term when he said: "I have been very jealous for the LORD, the God of hosts" (I Kings 19:10). Paul used the word in this same quite acceptable sense when he said to the Corinthian Christians: "I feel a divine jealousy for you" (II Corinthians 11:2).

There are two words in the Bible which are translated "jealous": the Hebrew *gana* and the Greek *zelos*. Both are also sometimes translated "zealous." When one is zealous about something, he is activated in its favor by an ultimate concern. It is precisely this meaning which is often intended when *gana* or *zelos* is translated "jealous." This is the meaning of the word which is intended when jealousy is attributed to God in the Second Commandment. It is the law of cause and effect which is affirmed. God ordained this law and by his authority it continues to operate. In keeping with its usual tendency to personalize all cosmic processes, Hebrew literary genius pictured God in the Second Commandment as personally manipulating the machinery of cause and effect. However one may visualize the actual working of this universal principle, the warning contained in this reference to it is clear: Those who allow any aid to worship to become an object of worship contribute to an impoverishment of life which is shared and suffered by all who come under its influence.

This fact as enunciated in the Second Commandment is balanced by the equally clear proclamation of the eternal availability of divine mercy. While the God who ordained both physical and moral law does not interfere in their working, he stands ever ready and able to bind up the hurts which man sustains in his rebellion against these laws, and to redeem him from ultimate destruction. The God who gave the law also gives grace by which the law may be fulfilled and by which man may be saved in spite of frequent failure in his effort to keep the law.

THE MORAL CHALLENGE OF THE SECOND COMMANDMENT

The prohibition against image-worship is not the final word of the Second Commandment. It is merely the initial and necessary bulldozing action which pushes aside the debris of moral and emotional confusion and prepares the way for a constructive appeal. God never ends any injunction on a negative note. He always proceeds beyond prohibition to point out a positive course of action. The positive appeal of the Second Commandment is a challenge to moral maturity. Obedience to the Second Commandment is no mere rejection of image-worship. It is the first step in such obedience. Full obedience to the Second Commandment consists in a never-ending process of growth toward moral maturity through a genuine and continuing experience of worship.

The Second Commandment presents God as the Creator and Ruler of the universe who because of his absolute sovereignty is able to deal mercifully and redemptively with man in his moral failure and defeat. The worship which the Second Commandment claims as due to God alone is presented as the experience in which man responds constructively to the sovereignty and the grace of God. Such worship results in an experience of spiritual growth by which man moves toward the realization of moral maturity. John Calvin was right in describing worship as "the first foundation of righteousness."[5] Worship is that centering of one's attention and affection on God which Von Ogden Vogt describes as "a deliberate turning of the mind away from all things as 'many' toward all things as 'One.' "[6] Worship, as B. E. Meland has pointed out, is the orientation of life around God as the center of being and the full commitment of the self to that center.

> Worship, taken as a phase of our total experience, is that rhythm in life which throws emphasis upon what is essential and of enduring significance to us. Worship is the *lunge toward reality*. It is the conscious effort to throw off the sham, the superficial, the trivial and sordid crustations that gather about us in daily associations. . . . It is

the recovery of basic patterns. It is adjustment of hopes
and habits. . . . Worship is full commitment to the sustaining forces in the universe, running through three stages:
awareness, reconciliation, and adjustment.[7]

In his book, *The Pipe of Desire and Other Plays,* George
Edward Barton tells the story of Klan who lived in the city of
Kaman in the land of Kaf. In his old age Klan took out the
image of his God whom he had served all his life, thanked him
for prospering him in so many ways, then announced that he
was going to fashion a larger image more worthy of the glory of
his God. The first stone he chose for this purpose was discarded
because it proved to be no larger than himself. After this disap-
pointment he began a search far and wide for something that
was worthy to be made into an image of his God. In this search
he was beseiged by every last thing in heaven and on earth,
clamoring loudly and persistently to be used as the image of his
God. The fuss and confusion of this experience was followed by
a period of utter silence out of which a quiet voice finally spoke
to Klan, saying: "Put me also into thy image of God." Now Klan
knew that he was at last in the presence of God himself, and
he took his old image from his bag and smashed it to bits on the
rock. Then Klan fell on his face and prayed before the God who
is God.[8]

This is the challenge of the Second Commandment—it challenges us to smash every image of anything in heaven or on the
earth which would usurp the place of God in our devotion. It
challenges us to that moral maturity that is achieved only in
the worship of the God who is God. This is the challenge which
Jesus reiterated when he said that "the hour is coming, and
now is, when the true worshipers will worship the Father in spirit
and truth, for such the Father seeks to worship him" (John 4:23).

III

THE INTEGRITY
OF MAN

The Third Commandment calls for sincerity and faithfulness in man's relationship with God. It recognizes the symbolic character of the name by which God is known, and forbids the hypocrisy which man practices when he accepts the name and rejects the Reality for which it stands. To take the name of God sincerely is to commit the self unreservedly to the will of God. The Third Commandment warns against the disintegration of personality which occurs inevitably when man takes God's name in vain—that is, when he verbally commits himself to God without accepting the will of God for his life.

THE SIGNIFICANCE OF THE NAME

A name is not nearly so important to us as it was to those who lived in more primitive times. Previously unimagined increases in populations and the consequent crowding together of many people who have no meaningful personal contact has greatly tended to reduce the significance we attach to a person's name. The endless duplication and registration of our names, necessitated by the complexities of our society and made possible by modern printing, typing, and filing devices, has minimized the role of the personal name as a living embodiment of a person's essential being. An individual's name is no longer a personal property; it is a public statistic. This changed status has lessened the prestige of the personal name and obscured its significance as the symbol which actually embodies the qualities and powers of the person to whom it belongs.

Modern man's narrowly circumscribed appreciation for the basic significance of a name has allowed him to see in the Third Commandment nothing more than a simple injunction against the irreverent use of God's name in speaking. Such an injunction, while altogether worthy in itself, is so lacking in that profound and universal moral concern which characterizes the other Commandments that it fails completely to challenge us in any decisive way whatever. Unconvinced that the Third Commandment is concerned solely with the petty offense of profanity, but unable to appreciate its true significance, we have held on to it as having some kind of antique value, while passing it by with only a reverent nod of recognition as being too trite or too vague to speak meaningfully to any important aspect of our contemporary moral problem.

To the Hebrews at the time the Ten Commandments were given, as to their contemporaries in other cultures, an individual's name nearly always had some definite and significant meaning. A person's name was never merely a combination of syllables to be pronounced as a means of getting his attention. The only son of Sarah, wife of Abraham was called "Isaac," which means "laughter," because his parents had first laughed in derision at God's promise to give them a son in their old age, then were caused to laugh with joy when this son was actually born to them (Genesis 17:17-19; 18:9-15; 21:1-6). One of Isaac's twin sons was called "Esau" ("hairy") because he was from birth more hairy than other boys.[1] "Samuel" means "asked of God." Hannah gave this name to her son because she believed God had given him to her in answer to her prayers for a child (I Samuel 1:20). Acting on this belief, she committed the child to the service of God when he was old enough to leave home, and the whole life of Samuel as prophet and judge of Israel became a living manifestation of the faith proclaimed in his name.

In this primitive culture a personal name was a living and potent symbol of the person who bore it. It was believed that an individual's name embodied much of the life and power and character of the person himself. A name was frequently employed as if it were actually the person to whom it was assigned, and the person so represented was expected to respond accordingly.[2]

While we are not now normally influenced in the selection of names for our children by the peculiarities of their physical appearance, or by particular events connected with their birth, the practice of naming things, particularly people, and the use and influence of names in human experience, are significant in any age. To name a thing is to endow it with certain qualities which it does not possess in an anonymous existence. For one thing, it becomes more easily recognizable. To name a thing is to give it a measure of individuality. A thing may possess individuality in itself, but that individuality is meaningful only to the degree that the thing itself is consciously aware of its own individuality and to the extent that its individuality is recognized by others. This is one of the things which is involved in being a person. The essence of personality is spirit. But to be a person, spirit must be particularized and identified. It must be individualized. It must be distinguished and distinguishable from other spirit. In short, it must be "personalized." It must be abstracted from spirit in general and become "a" spirit in particular. It must become consciously aware of itself as a spirit, an individual, a person, and perceptible to others as such. The assignment of a name alone does not accomplish this. Nomenclature is, however, an important part of the total process of individuation, the abstraction of the part from the whole, the identification of the "one" among the "many."

The need for a name with which man can pin down what he experiences as "God" is clearly evident. No absolutely satisfactory name for the Reality who demands and proves himself worthy of our supreme allegiance has ever been devised. From very early times God has been at least vaguely perceived as that One in whom "we live, and move, and have our being,"[3] and by whose power all things that are exist. This primitive experience of a Reality who is somehow the ground of all existence led to a pantheistic theology in which God was generally equated with the sum total of all being. As is nearly always the case, this pantheistic theology led to a polytheistic religion. When God is equated with the whole of things and is not distinguished from its parts, one may consistently worship the sun or the moon or a mountain or a graven image as his "god." Particular objects, specific parts of the "whole," however, very quickly take on a special character and significance in the affections of its devoted corps of worshipers. It is accorded a name, a dwelling place, and a particular order of worship. The part, which at first was revered only as a specific manifestation of the whole, very soon claims from its devotees the ultimate allegiance of which only the Center and Ground of the whole is worthy. Thus polytheism rapidly degenerates into mere idolatry.

When the Hebrews first became vaguely aware of the presence of a Being who is veritably the ground of all existence and at the same time distinguishable from any and all of its parts as a distinct, living, and purposefully ruling Personality, they were reluctant to assign to him any name at all. They hesitated to give a name to this Being whom they had encountered in experience because they found it difficult to devise a name suitable as a designation for the Reality they had come to know as worthy of their ultimate devotion. It was their custom, as we have noted, to name a thing in keeping with its character and power. The being and the power of this Reality, however, were too great to be comprehended, or even adequately suggested, by any name they knew. Furthermore, they were not at all sure that it would be safe for such a Being to be given a name which might become popularly known and used. Believing as they did that any name assigned to this Person would be invested, in part at least, with his tremendous power, they were loath to give him a name for fear that this power might be misdirected by those who might use his name improperly. When a name finally was assigned to him, therefore, it was the custom at first not to display it or pronounce it openly.

While the objections to the assignment of a name to the Reality whom the Hebrews had come to know as their "God" were strong, the need for it was even greater. A god who is not named is not God. Appellation does not endow anyone or anything with the character of Deity, but the being of God does require what is implied in the assignment of a name. The being of God requires individuality, abstraction, distinction. God, in order to be God, must be distinct from and independent of that which is not God. Furthermore, in order for God to be God in the awareness, loyalties, and affections of man, he must be distinguishable *to man* as such a distinct and independent Being. God in general is no God at all. Man cannot serve or worship an undistinguished and all-inclusive mass of being. In such a mass both his own and God's identity is lost. By definition one's "supreme" devotion, the devotion demanded by God, can be given only to a Being who is distinct and particular as over against other distinct beings to which it is not given, but to which something less than a supreme devotion is given.

While the Hebrews moved slowly in the process of naming the Divine Reality, God seems to have made a point of clearly identifying himself from the very beginning of his covenant relationship with them. He appeared personally to Abraham in Haran with instructions for his move to Canaan (Genesis 12:1-3). In subsequent encounters with this father of the faithful he identified himself as "the LORD who brought you from Ur of the Chaldeans, to give you this land to possess" (Genesis 15:7). He made himself known to Isaac as "the God of Abraham your father" (Genesis 26:24). To Jacob he revealed himself as "the LORD, the God of Abraham your father and the God of Isaac" (Genesis 28:13).

By the time of Moses the Israelites themselves had come to see how important it was that the Reality to whom they gave their supreme allegiance be distinguishable as One other than and superior to that which was not worthy of their ultimate devotion. In Egypt they had come in contact with those who worshiped the undistinguished whole of things, those who served every imaginable part of that whole, and others who had no idea what they were worshiping. In the religious consciousness of the Hebrews represented by Moses, there had emerged a clear if not consistently held conviction that no being is worthy of man's ultimate allegiance who is not other than and sovereign over everything else, and they insisted that the one to whom they gave their supreme devotion be identified as such a Person.

Because of this conviction Moses could be sure that in response to his call for an exodus from Egypt the Israelites would be sure to ask concerning the God who had promised to deliver them: "What is his name?" (Exodus 3:13.) The Israelites knew that from the moment they turned their backs on Pharaoh and the endless list of Egyptian deities in response to the promise of deliverance being offered by the God of their fathers they would be known by his name, bound in loyalty to him by this name, and that their destiny would depend upon the power of his Person as reflected in his name. For this reason they were greatly concerned about the identity of the God who offered to activate in their behalf the terms of the covenant made with their fathers, and it is on the basis of this significance which the name of God had for those to whom the Decalogue was given that we must understand the prohibition and the challenge of the Third Commandment as it applies to our own times and our own lives.

Taking the Name in Vain

We have pointed to the fact that what modern man has seen in the Third Commandment has been limited largely to a simple injunction against the impious use of God's name in speaking. Insofar as this view has encouraged respect for God and reverence in speaking his name we may be truly grateful for it. Few things are more distasteful to people of culture, or more offensive to refined sensibilities, than the injection of profanity of any kind into otherwise intelligent and meaningful discourse. The corruption of good manners by the use of vile language is all too common. With discouraging frequency, people who are sensitive to the demands of decency find themselves subjected to the unpleasantness of profane speech. It is particularly regrettable that conversation of this kind is being exploited commercially in many of our theaters. While no informed person would discourage realism in art, the now common practice of injecting pointless profanity into dramatic conversation for the sole purpose of creating a cheap sensation of shock cannot be too greatly deplored.

We make no mistake when we see in the Third Commandment a prohibition against the irreverent and improper speaking of God's name. We caricature the Commandment, however, and deprive it of its right to a place in the Decalogue when we interpret it and proclaim it as nothing more than a simple injunction against the impious pronunciation of the divine name. The Third Commandment was not given by a petulant God who is oversensitive to minor infractions of protocol in the speaking of his name. It was given by a loving God who is sympathetically sensitive to human need. The Third Commandment was designed not to protect the holiness of God, but to promote the integrity of man, and thus to make possible a mutually satisfying relationship between man and God.

"To take the name" is the phrase which was commonly used in ancient times to mean the taking of an oath in the name of any mutually accepted authority, such as a god, a king, an emperor, or a state. Bargains among the Hebrews were sealed in several ways. In certain cases an agreement was finalized when one party to the contract took off his shoe and gave it to the other (Ruth 4: 7-8). Agreements were sealed most commonly by an appeal to God, or to the name of God. Abraham executed a treaty of peace with Abimelech by swearing by God that he would keep its provisions (Genesis 21:23-24). To ensure a marriage between his son and a member of his own nation, Abraham made his chief lieutenant "swear by the LORD" that he would not allow Isaac to take a wife from among the Canaanites (Genesis 24:1-3). In the Deuteronomic exhortation the Israelites are commanded to fear the Lord, to serve him, and to "swear by his name" (Deuteronomy 6:13).

There are those who object strenuously to the use of God's name in taking an oath in court, or in any other situation, as being a "vain" use of the divine name. While this objection may be sustained on other grounds, it has little support in the sacred literature of the Hebrew-Christian tradition. In the bibli-

cal record God is represented not only as commanding the Hebrews to swear by his name but also as doing so himself. Re-
viewing events recorded in the Pentateuch (Genesis 22:15-18) the
author of Hebrews reports that "when God made a promise to
Abraham, since he had no one greater by whom to swear, he
swore by himself, saying, 'Surely I will bless you and multiply
you'" (Hebrews 6:13-14). According to the account of the
event given in Deuteronomy, it was with an oath also that God
sealed the covenant between himself and Israel of which the
Ten Commandments themselves form the basic structure. "You
stand this day all of you before the LORD your God; the heads of
your tribes, your elders, and your officers, all the men of Israel,
your little ones, your wives, and the sojourner who is in your
camp, both he who hews your wood and he who draws your
water, that you may enter into the sworn covenant of the LORD
your God, which the LORD your God makes with you this day"
(Deuteronomy 29:10-12).

Those who object to the use of God's name in taking an oath
base their objections for the most part on Jesus' words in the
Sermon on the Mount in which he said: "Again you have heard
that it was said to the men of old, 'You shall not swear falsely,
but shall perform to the Lord what you have sworn.' But I say
to you, Do not swear at all" (Matthew 5:33-34).

A careful reading of this passage, however, along with the
one on the same subject in the twenty-third chapter of Matthew,
reveals quite clearly the fact that what Jesus is concerned about
is not the use of God's name in the sincere swearing of an oath,
but the *insincere* use of God's name, or any other word, in the
taking of an oath by those who have no intention of keeping
their word when they give it. It was against the casuistries and
subterfuges of those who used oaths insincerely in order to
take advantage of others with whom they made a bargain that
Jesus spoke out. There were those in Jesus' day, for example,
who said, for reasons which best served their own selfish interests, that "If any one swears by the temple, it is nothing; but
if any one swears by the gold of the temple, he is bound by his
oath" (Matthew 23:16).

It was of such callous and hypocritical casuists that Jesus said: "You blind men! For which is greater, the gift or the altar that makes the gift sacred? So he who swears by the altar, swears by it and by everything on it; and he who swears by the temple, swears by it and by him who dwells in it" (Matthew 23:19-21).

It is true that in the Sermon on the Mount Jesus tried to show that men should live above the necessity for fortifying their words with oaths of any kind. This call to an ideal moral relationship among men on the part of Jesus can hardly be interpreted, however, to mean that a sincere and solemn employment of God's name in the taking of an oath constitutes a "vain," or profane use of it. What Jesus was concerned about, and what the Third Commandment is concerned about, is not the propriety of using the name of God in the taking of a serious and solemn oath, but the faithful keeping of the terms of the bargain into which a person enters by any means whatever, but particularly if he enters it by means of an appeal to the dignity and honor and authority of the divine name. As understood by the prophet Ezekiel, God's condemnation of the people of Jerusalem was not due to their using the name of God in taking an oath, but to the fact that they "despised the oath in breaking the covenant" (Ezekiel 16:59).

The relationship of God to the people to whom the Ten Commandments were given was a covenant relationship. In entering into this covenant the Hebrews "took the name of God" upon themselves. Both the Hebrews in taking the divine name upon themselves, and God in allowing them to take it, were bound by all the honor and authority and power of that name to keep the terms of the covenant into which they entered with one another. Failure on the part of either God or the Hebrews to live up to any of the terms of this covenant would be a falsification of everything represented by the divine name and a clear indication that the defaulting party had "taken the name in vain." This was the argument which Moses used to dissuade God from destroying the rebellious Israelites who refused to enter Canaan when they first reached its borders (Numbers 14: 11-19). Having agreed to follow God's leading when they entered into covenant with him (Exodus 19:3-9), the Israelites' refusal to obey God's command to enter Canaan at this time was a violation of the terms of the Covenant and a dishonor to the divine name. God, on the other hand, had represented himself as a merciful Deity (Exodus 20:5-6), and his refusal to deal patiently with his rebellious people, Moses reasoned, would have damaged his reputation and dishonored his name no less seriously than the defection of the Hebrews themselves.

For the people to whom the Third Commandment was first given, "to take the name of God in vain" was to fail to live up to the terms of any covenant entered into, or any agreement, promise, or profession made on the authority and honor of that name. This is what it means for us to take the name of God in vain. We take the name of God in vain when we profess to live in subjection to him as sovereign over our lives, then refuse to keep his commandments. We take God's name in vain when we call him Father and fail to give to him the honor and obedience which a child owes to his parent. We take God's name in vain when we call him our King, then forget or refuse to seek his Kingdom and his righteousness in the structuring and the operation of our social institutions. We take the name of God in vain when we say that we love him, but refuse to yield our lives to the guidance of his Holy Spirit.

We take the name of God in vain when we call ourselves "Christians," but make no serious effort to live in keeping with the example or teaching of Christ. When the Australian government took its latest census, 127,444 citizens said they were Baptists. This report was encouraging to the Baptists until a check on actual membership in the Baptist churches was made. A survey of Baptist church membership rolls in Australia turned up a total of only 37,841 names.[4] Somewhere in Australia there are more than eighty-nine thousand people who are taking the name of Baptists in vain. In claiming to be Baptists they also profess to be Christians, and in professing to be Christians without making any serious effort to live like Christians they are taking the name of God in vain.

Americans might not need to be so seriously concerned about

such insincerity in the taking of God's name if this moral hol-
lowness were confined to the Eastern Hemisphere, or even to
those who like to call themselves Baptists. Unfortunately, it is
not. A United States census survey conducted in March of 1957
revealed that in this country at that time there were 79 million
people who claimed to be Protestants, 30.7 million who professed
to be Roman Catholics, 3.9 million who called themselves Jews,
and 1.5 million who claimed some other religious loyalty. In spite
of the many remaining millions who profess no religious interest,
these are impressive figures. Research in urban areas where most
of those who are tabulated as having some religious affiliation are
now living indicate, however, that about 50% of those who
identified themselves as Protestants have no affiliation with a
local church, and in many instances don't even know the name
or location of a Protestant church. These surveys show that
about 65% of the self-identified Jews are that in ethnic heritage
only, and that approximately 35% of those who claimed to be
Roman Catholics do not accept the services of any local parish.[5]
It is possible, of course, that some of these who do not honor
the religious institutions to which they claim to belong by any
participation in their rites or services, may yet honor God by the
lives they live. Unfortunately, experience does not indicate
that this is so in any significant number of cases. The truth of
the matter is that those among the faithful church-goers who dishonor God's name by the kind of lives they live far outnumber
those among the negligent church members who honor God in
their day-by-day behavior.

We take the name of God in vain when we claim to have
divine approval and support for those of our own attitudes and
actions which are in obvious contradiction to the revealed nature
and will of God. The reputation of God and the influence of the
church in society have suffered immeasurably because as Christians we have indiscriminately claimed the authority and support
of God for cruel and needless wars of conquest, for irresponsible
and unneighborly foreign policies, for unscrupulous political
shenanigans, for indefensible class bigotry and race prejudice,
for dishonest business dealings, and for shameful religious

quackeries. The moral impact of the church in domestic affairs has been weakened almost to the vanishing point and our missionary enterprise abroad virtually defeated because we have used the divine name in support of social, economic, and political policies and practices which are not in keeping with divine principles or divine purposes. When Paul said to the Colossians: "Whatever you do, in word or deed, do everything in the name of the Lord Jesus," he did not mean that it was permissible for us to use the name of God to support any attitude or act of our own without regard to its moral character. He meant exactly the opposite. He meant that we should do only those things which are morally in keeping with the revealed nature and will of God, and in connection with which the name of God may be used with honor.

Taking the Name in Earnest

Although the Third Commandment is stated in negative terms, obedience to it involves more than a mere passive refusal to do something which is prohibited. The Decalogue is designed to give definite guidance to a *positive* way of life. The negative form in which most of these Commandments are cast is used in the interest of brevity, as it is in a great part of every legal code. Correct behavior can be outlined more easily by marking off the narrow strips of territory to be avoided than by specifying all of the many broad areas in which one may move with perfect propriety toward the fulfillment of his own life and in proper service to both God and man. Obedience to a negatively stated law does not consist wholly in passively keeping off forbidden territory, but also partly and mainly in exercising one's self in those areas where it is permissible, and by clear implication imperative, for him to act positively.

Obedience to the Third Commandment does not consist wholly in a mere passive refusal to take the name of God in vain. That is precisely what the greater part of the world's people are doing now, deliberately and quite consistently. They are refusing to take the name of God—in vain, or any other way.

They do not revile God. They simply ignore him. They are not impious toward God. They are just ignorant of God. Their sin is not blasphemy. It is blindness. They have no desire to take God's name in vain. They just want to forget it. They assume that by refusing to acknowledge the existence of God, they eliminate the Reality of God.

Of course the matter is not so simple as that. Just as we have seen that we do not bring a reality into being by merely naming it, we also do not eliminate a reality from existence by simply refusing to name it. The particular name by which we may designate the Reality we experience and commonly call "God" is not important. The intellectual forms by which we conceive of him are important only to the extent that they enable us to relate ourselves properly to him. That we experience, acknowledge, and yield ourselves to the sovereign rule and creative working of this Reality in our lives is all-important. This Reality is experienced as Creative Good, Forgiving Love, Redemptive Grace, Eternal Justice, Perfect Righteousness, the Process of Spiritual (Conscious, Personal) Growth Toward the Fulfillment of All the Ends of Being. This is at least a part of what we mean to indicate when we use the simple word "God." Obedience to the Third Commandment requires not only that we not ignore or speak evil of this Reality but that we also acknowledge his sovereignty over us and respond positively and affirmatively to his working in our lives.

This fact is of the utmost importance to our understanding of and obedience to the Third Commandment. We have seen that this Commandment was meaningful to the Hebrews primarily in terms of their Covenant relationship with God. When they entered into covenant with God, they took the name of God upon themselves, and from that point on any aspect of their behavior which was not in keeping with the nature and will of God constituted a "vain" (false, dishonoring, defamatory) use, or "taking," of the divine name. But while the terms of the Covenant were explained to the Hebrews and willingly accepted by them, there is no indication that they had any real choice in the matter. They had a choice of living co-operatively with God in obedience to the terms of the Covenant, or trying to live without God and without obedience to the terms of the Covenant. But this was only a choice between life and death, as is clearly stated in the Deuternomic review of the terms and meaning of the Covenant (Deuteronomy 30:11-20). By its very nature the Covenant was one which could not be rejected without rejecting life itself. And while, according to Hebrew tradition, the Covenant was made originally with only one nation, from the beginning it was designed ultimately to include the whole human race (Genesis 12:1-3). Indeed, there never was and never can be any immunity from the working of the moral law for any part of the human race. When the "heathen" nations who never took the name of the God of Israel upon themselves and made no pretense of serving him as their God defied the moral law, they destroyed themselves no less quickly and completely than the Hebrews who took the name of God "in vain." The ritual requirements and provincial laws contained in the Covenant with Israel had only a local and quite temporal reference, but the moral laws which it emphasized, such as those enunciated in the Decalogue, are binding on all men at all times. The Covenant was not a means of bringing anyone under the moral law. All men are at all times subject to that law. The Covenant was a means of making the moral law obvious, and a means of bringing man to an acceptance of that divine grace by which alone he is able to come to terms with moral law.

We do not escape the demands of the Third Commandment by refusing to use the name of God at all, or by refusing to acknowledge the existence of the Reality which it designates. The Third Commandment is either one of the moral laws by which the universe is eternally ordered, or a preposterous and immoral attempt to impose an antiquated and irrelevant tribal taboo on the whole body of mankind. It either applies to all of us at all times, or to none of us at any time. It is a categorical imperative, or it is nothing.

The Third Commandment rests squarely on the Hebrew doctrine of man's creation in the image of God. It is the logical and inevitable corollary to the Hebrew concept of the Fatherhood of God. The Covenant relationship with Israel was simply a symbolic schooling experience which revealed by means of a concrete historic demonstration the Father-child relationship which exists between God and all his human creatures. Whether we like it or not, we have all "taken the name" of God. We are all his children, whether we want it so or not. If we keep the terms of this universal covenant, that is, if we live up to our sonship in obeying the will of our Father, we experience the fulfillment of our lives in terms of the nature of our being as sons of God. If we "take the name of God in vain," that is, if we deny our sonship and rebel against the very nature of our being in disobedience to the will of God for our lives, we destroy ourselves. This is the sense in which we are to understand the harsh-sounding phrase in the Third Commandment which declares that "God will not hold him guiltless that taketh his name in vain." What we have here is not a God who like an exasperated drill sergeant slaps down those who get out of line, but a just and loving God who will not remove the guideposts which point us to the realization of our sonship, even though some of us insist on crushing our spiritual being by rebelliously casting ourselves against them.

The tendency to ignore the demands of the Third Commandment is unfortunately as strong among those who take the name of God as among those who deny it, and much more damaging to the moral health of the human race. Those who reject the will of God over their lives without pretending that he is their God are guilty of disobedience, but there is at least an element of honesty in the forthrightness of their rebellion. But when those who "take the name of God"—that is, those who profess that they are the children of God—reject God's will over their lives, they are guilty of both disobedience and insincerity. This is the tragedy of the religious community against which the Third Commandment warns us: the tragedy of taking the name of God in word and in the observance of religious rites while denying and desecrating it in our deeds. This is the bifurcated, schizophrenic kind of behavior which Jesus denounced as hypocrisy. It is the deadliest sin in the catalogue of human errors. The hypocrite, the religious person who praises God with his lips on Sunday only to dishonor him with his life on Monday, not only defiles his own character but also discourages those who might be inclined toward a sincere relationship with God and their fellowmen. It was against those who thus take the name of God in vain that Jesus inveighed when he said: "But woe to you, scribes and Pharisees, hypocrites! because you shut the kingdom of heaven against men; for you neither enter yourselves, nor allow those who would enter to go in . . . you traverse sea and land to make a single proselyte, and when he becomes a proselyte, you make him twice as much a child of hell as yourselves" (Matthew 23:13, 15).

What the Third Commandment calls for is integrity. It asks that a man's profession be substantiated by his performance. This is what Joshua called for when he exhorted the Israelites to "fear the Lord, and serve him in sincerity and in faithfulness" (Joshua 24:14). It is what the author of I John asked of the early Christians when he said: "Little children, let us not love in word or speech but in deed and in truth" (I John 3:18). Integrity—the correspondence of profession with performance, conformity on the part of the child to the image of the Father which is stamped in the very nature of his being—is what Jesus asked of all men when he said to them: "Love your enemies and pray for those who persecute you, so that you may be sons of your Father who is in heaven" (Matthew 5:44-45).

Mencius was right. "Sincerity is the way of Heaven."[6] But it is not an easy way. A sincere life is an open challenge to the pretentious powers of evil. Sincerity exposes the hypocritical and irritates the indolent and complacent. Integrity of life and character landed Jesus on a cross. He could hold out no better prospect to those who would be his disciples. Sincerity is nothing less than the willingness to sacrifice one's self in devotion to what he believes to be right and of supreme value. James Russell Lowell put the matter strongly but nonetheless accurately when he said that "the only conclusive evidence of a man's sincerity is that he give *himself* for a principle."[7] This is what the Christ asks of those who would take his name. "If any one comes to me and does not hate his own father and mother and wife and children and brothers and sisters, yes, and even his own life, he cannot be my disciple" (Luke 14:26).

This is the kind of sincerity in taking the name of God that the Third Commandment asks of all men.

IV

THE RHYTHM
OF LIFE

When a typically overtaxed New York theatrical producer said to Herman Wouk: "I don't envy you your religion, but I envy you your Sabbath,"[1] he expressed the deeply felt if not so frankly confessed sentiment of our whole harried, hurried, confused, and fumbling world.

Many of us today are much too sophisticated to feel a need for any kind of religion. We have outgrown in turn our tribal taboos, our primitive superstitions, *and* our religious faith. But we have not outgrown our human nature. We have not outgrown the need for those disciplines by which our lives may be regulated in keeping with the nature of our own being.

Perhaps we can dispense with some of the formalities of religion. If human life is to survive and be fulfilled, we cannot dispense with those disciplines—call them "religious" or not— which are demanded by the very nature of man's being. One of those disciplines is the rhythmic alternation of properly proportioned periods of activity and quiescence.

How We Got Our Sabbath

Like many of the other disciplines which we find to be imperative today, our modern practice of Sabbath observance has roots which reach far back into the religious experience of ancient Israel. One of the earliest references to the institution of the Sabbath in Hebrew history is found in the Exodus version of the

Decalogue. Here the observance of a Sabbath, or rest period, on the seventh day of every week is enjoined as a reverent acknowledgment of God's creative activity in making the world in six days and his sovereign decision to rest on the seventh. As it appears in Exodus the Fourth Commandment calls for the observance of the Sabbath in imitation of what was believed to be the divine example and in keeping with the obvious belief that by this example God had set aside the seventh day to be observed perpetually as a day of rest for both man and beast. In this tradition the memorial character of the Sabbath is clear. The Sabbath is to be remembered and observed as being in itself a reminder of the fact that God is the ground and source of all being and that his example is to be followed and his commandments obeyed (Exodus 20:8-11).

In the Deuteronomic version of the Fourth Commandment the memorial significance of the Sabbath is retained, but the reference is entirely different. According to the Fourth Commandment as it appears in Deuteronomy, a Sabbath is to be observed on the last day of every week as a reminder to the Hebrews that God had delivered them from the bondage of Egypt. There is no explicit mention here of God's creation of the world in six days or his rest on the seventh.

In the Deuteronomic version of the Fourth Commandment, which is probably a later reflection on the one which appears in Exodus, a humanitarian concern is made explicit, but the day which is to be kept holy is still "the sabbath to the LORD your God." The humanitarian appeal in the Commandment is strengthened by a reminder to the Hebrews that at one time in Egypt they themselves were subjected to the destructive effects of uninterrupted slave labor. At the same time they are reminded that it was God who delivered them from this bondage, and that because of the sovereign power displayed in that act, he has the authority to command them to keep the Sabbath and to extend the privilege of keeping it to everyone under their direction (Deuteronomy 5:12-15).

In its earliest forms the Sabbath as observed among the Hebrews does not seem to have been marked by any kind of formal worship. It was essentially a day of rest for both mind and body. At no time, however, was it without significant religious implications. From its earliest appearances in the post-Exodus life of Israel, Sabbath observance was also an acknowledgment of the sovereignty of God in both his creative activity and his redemptive outreach, and such an acknowledgment is in itself an act of religious significance.

Through the centuries the influence of the Sabbath—as a humanitarian social custom and as a religious institution—increased steadily until it became what one Jewish scholar has described as "the most vital force in Jewish life and theology."[2] Among Hebrew institutions it is regarded as being equal in importance to the commandments and circumcision.

The Jewish Sabbath and the Christian Sunday are marked by distinct differences, but they are not without very definite connections—both historical and theological. For both Jew and Christian the observance of the Sabbath is an acknowledgment of divine sovereignty. For both it is an expression of humanitarian concern for human well-being; it is a day of rest. For both—now and at the time Christianity adopted the practice—it is a day of worship. For both it is a memorial institution. For the Jews it is a memorial to the work and rest of God in the creation and contemplation of the universe, and a memorial to the redemptive act of God in delivering the Israelites from Egyptian bondage. For the Christian it is a memorial to the resurrection of Jesus Christ. The Jew, therefore, observes the Sabbath on the last day of the week because it was on that day that God is believed to have rested after the creation of the world. The Christian observes the Sabbath on the first day of the week because it is to that day that the resurrection of Jesus is attributed.

The change from Saturday to Sunday as the day on which the Christian community came to observe the Sabbath was not made suddenly. Jesus followed the traditional Jewish custom of observing the Sabbath on the seventh day of the week and most likely never dreamed of its being changed to any other day. The only fault Jesus ever found with the Jewish Sabbath was the Pharisees' abuse of it in making it a burden to man rather than a help as it was intended to be.

Paul's attitude toward Sabbath observance on any day of the week seems to have been one of indifference, theologically (Colossians 2:16-17; Romans 14:5-6), but as a matter of practical convenience he commonly worshiped and preached on the seventh day of the week (Acts 15:21; 18:4). While many of the Jews who embraced Christianity in its early days undoubtedly continued to observe the traditional Sabbath customs, Jewish Sabbath legislation was not considered by the church to be binding on Christians generally (Acts 15:23-29). As Judaism became more violent in its opposition to Christianity, and as Christians became more conscious of their existence as a distinct religious community, they turned deliberately to the first day of the week as the time for their weekly worship in honor of their risen Lord and as a distinguishing feature of their religious fellowship.

As Christianity slowly gained status as a legal and then as an official state religion, civil and ecclesiastical legislation was enacted to enforce strict observance of the Christian Sabbath. It was at this point that the Christian "Lord's Day" assumed the definite characteristics of a day of rest as well as a day of worship. In 321, plagued with the endless number of holy days observed by the various sects in his domain, the Emperor Constantine issued a decree which made Sunday a day of rest from all general labor. While the choice of Sunday as the official day of rest was certainly influenced by Constantine's Christian sympathies, it was selected also because it was a day which most of the other factions in the Empire could agree to observe also.

THE SABBATH PRINCIPLE AND THE NATURE OF MAN

To understand *how* we got our Sabbath is not enough. We need to understand also *why* we got it and why it is imperative that we continue to keep it. The Sabbath cannot escape the pragmatic test to which all principles and practices are now subjected. To exempt the Sabbath from this test is to admit its lack of vital worth.

What we claim for the Fourth Commandment is the universal obedience which man owes to every moral law. This claim rests on the conviction that Sabbath observance is demanded by necessities which are inherent in the very nature of man's own being.

The necessity of man's nature which demands a pattern of existence approximated in Sabbath observance is rooted in the rhythmic character of the life process in which his being consists. Life does not flow in a steady stream. It pulsates. Being is neither static sameness nor erratic change. It is the rhythmic throbbing of the heart of God. The rise and fall of the tides, the alternation of light and darkness, and the ceaseless cycle of the seasons with its alternate periods of productivity and quiescence, all bear witness to the fact that life does not move toward its ultimate goal at an even and uninterrupted pace. Life on every plane below the voluntary exercise of human freedom is regulated inexorably in accordance with a rhythmic pattern of activity and rest. Being at every level is characterized by steeps and plateaus, steps and stops.

A clear reflection of the rhythmic character of all life may be seen in the use of rhythm in certain types of artistic expression. The basic aim of art in all its varied forms is to express and interpret reality. Obviously, such expression can be given most effectively in terms of the nature of reality itself. The use of rhythm in several of the arts (e.g., music, poetry, and dancing) is an application of this principle. Rhythm was not invented arbitrarily as a method of artistic expression. Rather, rhythm was discovered to be a vital part of the life process and was adopted by practitioners of certain of the arts as one means of expressing and interpreting reality.

Because all else comes under the direction of the inexorable laws of nature, no form of life ever suffers from a violation of this principle of rhythm in being except man, or animals with whose natural pattern of behavior man has interfered. A tree cannot decide to keep on bearing leaves and fruit through the cold, hard months of winter with no time out for rest. It has no such freedom of choice or action. But a man can continue to drive his mind and body long after those organisms have passed the point of needed rest and recreation. Thus, because there is in human experience an area of choice and action which is not automatically or arbitrarily regulated by the laws of nature, man stands constantly in danger of self-destruction. And in recognition of this danger God has revealed to man certain moral laws by the observance of which he may avoid the pitfalls that are ever before him in the exercise of human freedom. The Fourth Commandment is one of these moral laws; i.e., one of the laws of nature which operate in the realm of freedom.

The moral and therefore universal character of the Sabbath observance requirement as being rooted in the necessities of human nature itself is indicated by the occurrence of a work-rest rhythm in almost every one of the widely scattered cultures which make up the society of man. In tracing the steps by which we got *our* Sabbath we mentioned only the Hebrew and Christian traditions in which we stand, but Sabbath observance—or some rhythmic alternation of periods of activity and repose approximating it—has by no means been confined to Judeo-Christian civilizations. If exceptions be made of the Australian, Melanesian, and American areas, it may be said that the observance of rest days intervening between longer periods of work forms a remarkably common custom among the lower cultures of mankind. What might be called primitive Sabbaths have been observed widely as an important part of Polynesian life, for example, especially on the island of Hawaii. These peoples observed four rest days—or *taboo* periods—in every lunar month, an arrangement which significantly approximates the Hebrew and Christian work-rest cycles. Paralleling the Hebrew-Christian practice of Sabbath observance, but having no causative connection with it, is the Buddhist *Uposatha* which customarily falls on the day of the new moon, and the day of the full moon, and on the two days which are eighth from the new and the full moon, and which is observed by fasting and the interruption of all secular activities.[3] The Babylonians also had a calendar of feasts and sacrifices in accordance with which the seventh, fourteenth, twenty-first, and twenty-eighth days of every month were set apart as periods during which no work was to be done.[4]

Modern attempts to eliminate Sabbath observance or radically alter its primitive time cycle have ended in either failure or disaster. During the period of her great eighteenth-century revolution, when the nation's political leaders were making a deliberate effort to break all the customary ties with religious institutions, France undertook to abolish the weekly Sabbath and substitute a rest day which would occur once in every ten days. This experiment worked so disastrously that in spite of their antireligious sentiments the officials of the country had to return to the observance of a weekly Sabbath.[5]

No human need, not even one among those common to all men, ever occurs in *exactly* the same rhythm or intensity in *every* person. It is very likely that the work-rest pattern of life needed by every human being varies considerably from one individual to another. It is entirely possible that people generally might get along fairly well on a six or an eight day work-rest cycle. Experience no less than revelation strongly indicates, however, that a work-rest cycle closely approximating the weekly Sabbath pattern is a requirement rooted in the very nature of man's being.

In experiments made two generations ago, Dr. Haegler of Switzerland discovered that more oxygen is expended by the human body in a day of toil than is recovered in a night of rest. The weekly Sabbath is necessary to restore the cumulative losses of six days of labor.[6] What is true of man's physical body in this respect is true of his being as a whole. A man's loss of spiritual energy during a day of activity can be restored no more completely in a night of rest than his loss of physical energy. Bearing within himself the image of the divine Spirit as well that of a physical body, restorative rest for the whole of man's being requires not only cessation of labor but also communion with God. The weekly Sabbath serves its purpose, therefore, not merely in its use as a day of physical repose, but also in its use as a day of worship.

Sabbath Observance and Economic Necessity

If the validity of Sabbath observance rests on the existence of a human need rooted in the rhythmic character of the life process in which man shares, keeping one's self constructively occupied during the work periods which separate the rest days is as much a moral demand as the Sabbath requirement itself. The occupation of one's self in a period of useful labor as a necessary complement to the observance of a periodic day of rest is implied in every mention of the weekly Sabbath in the Hebrew-Christian tradition and explicitly required in the Fourth Commandment. Apart from being an economic necessity, several days of constructive activity between every regularly spaced day of rest is essential to the health of the whole man as a single, unified personality. Efficient employment is impossible without properly spaced periods of rest. Rest is impossible without a prior period of constructive employment of sufficient duration and intensity.

In cultures where slave laborers or arbitrarily employed people are compelled to meet all of the work requirements of a society, the danger is that those who labor will be required to work too long and rest too little. In a free society, such as that which exists in this country, there is as much danger that many of us will work too little as there is that we will work too much. The Fourth Commandment is designed to guard against both of these dangerous extremes by keeping the natural work-rest rhythm of life in proper balance in human experience.

In America, where the productive aspect of the economy is adequately mechanized and efficiently operated, there has been no problem in recent years of ability to produce the goods and services sufficient to supply the needs of the whole population on the basis of a six-day work week. Ostensibly, the problem has been one of *over* production. What *appears* to be a surplus of goods on the market frequently reduces, or threatens to reduce, the rewards of production (income) below the level necessary to keep the wheels of industry turning. Consequently, in an effort to drain this supposed surplus of goods off the market, we have made a five-day work week mandatory for a large proportion of our people. The question now arises as to whether or not this five-day work week violates that part of the Fourth Commandment which calls for six days of labor prior to the weekly day of rest.

In answer to this question two things need to be made clear.

In the first place, our problem up to this point is not one of over production. It is a problem of inadequate distribution. We have developed the capacity to produce a supply of goods and services sufficient to meet the needs of all our people, but we have not yet devised means of distributing this possible sufficiency of goods to all our people which are in keeping with the political and economic concepts of freedom which we hold, and which are able at the same time to keep production at the needed level. In addition to the need for such means of distribution in our domestic economy, there is the even greater need for means whereby our productive capacity may be applied to the immeasurably immense task of helping to supply the desperately urgent economic needs of millions of virtually destitute people in other lands. In the Hebrew-Christian cultural and religious tradition, it is required that a man work not only to supply the necessities of life for himself but also "that he may be able to give to [*metadidonai*, "share with"] those in need" (Ephesians 4:28). If economically and politically feasible means of distributing the fruits of production to meet the economic needs of *all* the world's people were devised, it is possible that the need for a six-day work week envisioned in the Fourth Commandment would continue to hold, if not permanently at least for the immediate future.

It is conceivable, of course, that, even when our productive capacity is put to work helping to supply all human needs, the task may be accomplished in something less than a six-day work week. A five-day or even a four-day work week, if with the help of improved machines and methods of production the task of supplying the economic needs of the world can be accomplished in some such shorter period, does not constitute a violation of any part of the Fourth Commandment. What this Commandment calls for is not a six-day work week which is necessarily devoted entirely to the production of goods and services, or to any kind of formal employment or income-earning activity, but six days of every week devoted to doing "*all* thy work."

"All" the work which man needs to do is not included in the effort required to produce the goods and services essential to mere existence. Man—man as anything more than a well-fed animal—does not live by bread alone. In his effort to realize the full potentialities of his being as a person made in the image of God, man needs to do many things which can only be described as "work" and do not fit into any day devoted to rest and worship, but which also do not fit into the necessarily rigid economic pattern of any formal business enterprise. Man—every man—needs to think, study, travel, communicate with others, and create and cultivate new and more satisfying ways of enriching and enjoying his existence as a human being in relationship with other human beings. These activities, no less than those devoted to the production of goods and services required to supply our more elemental needs, come under the heading of "work," and any possible shortening of the necessary productive, income-earning work week which will give the common man more time for this creative and culturally enriching kind of work should be understood not as a violation of the Fourth Commandment but as a valuable opportunity for human development. The Fourth Commandment is violated only when this extra time provided by a shorter compulsory work week is spent in idleness or harmful pursuits, rather than in creative work of a voluntary and wisely directed nature.

Sabbath Legislation in a Pluralistic Society

Because a rhythmic work-rest cycle such as that required by the Fourth Commandment is a necessity of human nature itself, the requirement that it be observed must be understood as having the character and force of natural law, and would therefore seem to be a proper subject for civil legislation. While it is true that the force of most natural laws having to do with human behavior —that is to say, most moral laws—may and ought to be brought to bear on man's behavior as a member of society in terms of human law, not every such natural law can be effectively implemented by means of civil legislation.

The most nearly satisfactory theory with regard to the expediency of implementing moral law by means of civil legislation is the one which holds that government may enact and enforce laws pertaining to moral concerns, but none having to do with religious concerns. This is the theory on which the religion clause in the first amendment to our national constitution rests. The weakness of this theory in practice lies in the close—sometimes almost inseparable—relatedness of moral law to religious discipline. While there are religious requirements—mere cultic practices— which as such have no particular moral implications, there are no moral laws which are not also a concern of religion. This inevitable intermixture of moral law and religious discipline poses a serious but not altogether insuperable legislative problem. It is the problem of covering the whole field of moral concern with adequate civil legislation without trespassing in the area of religion.

Properly understood and applied, the religion clause in the first amendment to our national constitution—"Congress shall make no law respecting an establishment of religion, or prohibiting the free exercise thereof"—goes a long way toward providing a sound basis for at least a partial solution to this knotty problem. This constitutional provision means that the government cannot make any law which in effect favors, supports, or discriminates against any religious institution or cultic discipline, even though the primary function of such a religious institution or cultic discipline is to implement—that is, obtain obedience to—a moral law. The religion clause in the first amendment does not mean that government cannot pass and enforce civil laws designed to implement moral laws if in the nature of the case it is possible and practicable to do so, even though such moral laws are also religious principles.

For example, the Commandment, "Thou shalt not kill," is a natural moral law; but it is at the same time most certainly also a law of religion. Nevertheless, the fact that this is a religious law as well as a moral law does not prevent the government from passing and enforcing civil laws against murder. On the other hand, among our various religious groups Bible study, prayer, worship, church attendance, and church membership are all religious disciplines, or cultic practices, designed and prescribed by

the church or other religious institutions to implement obedience
to the moral law, "Thou shalt not kill," along with others like it.
What the religion clause in our constitution prohibits is enactment and enforcement by government of any law which in effect
favors, supports, or discriminates against any such purely religious
discipline or cultic practice.

For the legislator, the problem is how to implement natural
moral laws in a given society by means of civil legislation without
favoring or discriminating against any of the existing religious
institutions and cultic disciplines, most of which are designed to
serve the same end. The problem is simplified with regard to certain moral laws because, in these cases, no effective civil legislation is possible. For example, the Commandment, "You shall not
covet . . ." is a moral law to which obedience may be encouraged
by religious disciplines and cultic practices, but which cannot be
implemented in terms of civil legislation. The whole category
of human desires and inwardly rooted motivations, while it is a
legitimate concern of government, is simply too deeply seated
within the self to be effectively touched by civil legislation. The
best that government can do at this point is to take into consideration the presence and possible effects of these inner attitudes
in applying the laws which bear on our more overt experiences.

Other moral laws are outside, or partly outside, the area of
effective civil legislation, not because it is impossible to enact
effective civil legislation pertaining to them but because such
legislation is not politically expedient. The First and Second
Commandments calling for the acceptance of only one particular
God and forbidding the worship of anything which is not this
God are clearly moral laws which can be translated into quite
definite forms of civil legislation. However, the religious aspect
of these laws is so strong and so closely intertwined with the
moral that civil enforcement of them as mere moral precepts is
politically impracticable. Furthermore, the interpretations placed
on the religious aspect of these laws—and the reaction to them—
on the part of religious enthusiasts themselves, as well as others,
are so diverse and frequently so contradictory as to make successful civil legislation in this field practically impossible. For these

reasons, in such areas of inseparable relationship between moral and cultic concerns, and where many conflicting opinions are hopelessly divided, government is wisely restricted to the enactment of only permissive and protective legislation such as that in the first amendment to our national constitution which proclaims a policy of noninterference on the part of government in the cultic affairs of religion and guarantees to all alike the right to engage in religious exercises on a voluntary and privately supported basis.

The Fourth Commandment is clearly among those moral laws which, while they are in themselves proper subjects for civil legislation, are so closely related to such a wide variety of conflicting religious customs and cultic practices as to make it politically impractical to attempt to implement them by means of any kind of direct legal action. What this boils down to is the hard, cold fact that in a pluralistic society—and all societies are pluralistic to some extent—Sabbath observance, as imperative and as morally significant as it is, must be sustained solely by personal conviction and commitment aided by religious custom and teaching. This has been a hard lesson for both legislators and Christian Sabbath enthusiasts. In spite of the painful promptings of experience in the field of Sabbath legislation from the time of Constantine to the present, few of us are yet ready to accept this truth. But truth does not wait for our readiness. Our political hope lies today in the democratic process. There is no place in this process for any legislative support for any religious discipline, however closely or beneficially it may be related to a moral law. On humanitarian grounds government can legislate one day of rest in seven for most employees, but that is as far as it can go. In a pluralistic society such as ours, it has no constitutional or moral right to designate any one particular day for such rest, or to prescribe how it shall be used, other than prohibiting its use for work at one's usual occupation.[7]

THE PRACTICE OF THE SABBATH PRINCIPLE IN THE MODERN WORLD

Sabbath observance in this country has already been deprived of many of is legislative props, and the prospect for the future is that it will eventually lose all of its legal sanctions except those which are only permissive and protective and those with a purely humanitarian reference.[8] In addition to this rapidly changing legal status of the Sabbath, the person who would observe it today, as over against those who have honored it in other ages, is faced also with a radically different kind of civilization. While this new and different cultural situation may require adjustment in our thinking about the Sabbath principle, it does not make a satisfying practice of it impossible.

The first step we need to take if we are going to make any serious effort to practice the Sabbath principle in the modern world is to stop relying on legislative supports and accept the fact that the responsibility for Sabbath observance must be borne on a voluntary basis by the individual, the family, and by the religious and business institutions involved. With regard to Sabbath observance as such, all we can hope for and all we have a right to expect from government is permissive and protective legislation and the same voluntary co-operation with regard to its own employees that we might expect from any other employer. This is not much, but it is enough. The Jews have kept their seventh-day Sabbath with notable success for thousands of years in practically every kind of culture, most of the time without benefit of any legislative assistance. Certainly Christians should ask no more, and do no less. It is not only possible to practice the Sabbath principle without more legislative support than we have a right to expect, but also probable that Sabbath observance on this basis will be much more rewarding in terms of the full development of human personality than on any other.

Another adjustment essential to any realistic attempt to practice the Sabbath principle today is to get away from the idea that the Sabbath can or necessarily should be observed on the same day of the week by every member of a modern society. A single, unanimously accepted day for rest and worship may be the most desirable arrangement for Sabbath observance, and it may be possible in a simple agrarian culture, but it is very unlikely that this ideal can be reached in any complex, industrialized, and technologically developed society such as we have in America. Our modern medical and hospital care, our police and fire protection requirements, our transportation and communication systems, our utility services, and many aspects of our productive and public services economy make it absolutely necessary that large numbers of people be at work on every day of the week. This does not mean that any person need be denied a weekly day away from work which can be devoted to rest and worship. It simply means that not all of us can observe the Sabbath on the same day of the week. This necessity of modern society does not affect the rest aspect of the Sabbath, but it does pose a problem for public worship in the case of those whose weekly time away from work falls on a day other than the one which the religious community to which he belongs normally conducts services of public worship. The problem is not too serious. It is being solved already in urban and industrial areas, where the problem is most acute, by churches which have introduced regular services of worship on days other than Sunday.

The complexities of modern society also make any list of "do's" and "don'ts" for Sabbath observance which would be useful on any wide scale extremely difficult to compile. To say that what we should strive for one day in seven as a "Sabbath" in the full sense of rest for body and mind from one's normal occupation and of spiritual renewal through worship in reverent and grateful communion with God in company with one's fellowman is perhaps sufficient. The day is also a time for the strengthening of family ties in an atmosphere of relaxed fellowship and unhurried contemplation of God's Word and God's will for our lives.

V

THE CONTINUITY
OF LIFE

Viewed in the light of the present situation the Fifth Commandment is the bravest in the whole catalogue of moral legislation. It actually imposes a duty on *children!* If it had originated in this generation, there could be no question of divine authorship. No one else today would dare address Junior in the imperative mood.

Although the Fifth Commandment is directed specifically toward children (of all ages), it is not on that account discriminatory or limited in the scope of its application. It is precisely in this orientation toward the child-role (discipleship) in human experience that its universal character is most apparent. For while it is not the privilege of all of us to *be* parents, all of us *have* parents, and all of us alike are dependent upon our predecessors for the cultural foundation on which our own civilization must be built.

The duty which the Fifth Commandment imposes on all human beings is the all-inclusive and absolutely indispensable obligation to assimilate and use diligently and wisely the store of cultural values accumulated by society as a result of the successive experiences of previous generations. This can be accomplished only in an atmosphere of proper reverence on the part of each succeeding generation for those which have come before it. Such a fitting regard for the achievements of the past in the affairs of the present is what the Fifth Commandment requires.

HISTORY AND HUMAN DESTINY

The call for a conscious and co-operative response to the values hammered out on the hard anvil of human experience is based on a principle of life which is inherent in the nature of man's own being. *It is the principle of growth under the conditions of limited constraint and limited freedom.* Life at every level is subject to these conditions. At the lower levels, where consciousness, thought, and feeling are absent or practically absent, life is characterized by a high degree of external determination. The routine of existence and reproduction is followed instinctively without any consciousness of ends or effort at improvement. Deviations from this routine are either fortuitous or forced by environmental changes and may be somewhat progressive, inconsequential, or fatal. Except where their development is directed by some outside intelligence—as in agriculture and husbandry—such forms of life normally reach a certain level of existence and remain stationary, or decline if called upon to make adjustments which require any considerable degree of flexibility.

The character and destiny of life at this level is determined almost entirely by the forces of heredity and environment. Since consciousness and intellectual activity exist only at a minimal level, if at all, there is no retentiveness of any significance, and therefore nothing of importance is ever learned from experience. Such forms of life have less freedom than those in which intellect is more highly developed, and are therefore less likely to destroy themselves through any misuse of freedom. On the other hand, however, since they learn nothing from past experience they are doomed to an endless repetition of it, and to extinction when confronted with changed enviromental conditions which require a drastic change in the routine of existence they follow.

To a certain extent human life is circumscribed by the same determinations of heredity and environment by which life at the lower levels is characterized. However, because of his superior intellect and the much greater degree of freedom which he has, man is able to learn from experience, appropriate the accumulated values of the past, control his environment to an appreciable extent, and by these means to exercise a substantial influence on the development of his own character and the shaping of his own destiny. On the other hand, his possession of these superior capacities, particularly his vastly greater freedom of choice and action, greatly increase for him the possibility and danger of self-destruction.

What this amounts to is the fact of man's responsibility for his own personal development and the development of civilization in keeping with the highest potentialities of his nature. To the extent of their capabilities lower forms of life respond instinctively to the possibilities which heredity and environment offer them. They can do neither more nor less. In order to make the most of what heredity and environment hold out to him, man has to make a deliberate personal effort. Within certain limitations he is free to assimilate and use the best that past experience has to offer in the development of his own personality and the improvement of his civilization. He is equally free to neglect the hard-won heritage of the past and let himself and his culture fall into decay. The choice is entirely his own. He is forced by no irresistible instincts to make even a minimal response to the opportunities for self-fulfillment which are open to him.

These facts indicate clearly that the Fifth Commandment has the character of a natural moral law. Moral laws are never enforceable except by the one to whom they apply, and by him only for himself. There can be no arbitrary enforcement of moral law as such because moral laws apply only to those who are free to obey or rebel. There is no punishment for rebellion against a moral law except the forfeiture of that fulfillment of one's potentialities which is the only reward of obedience.

While man—because of his superior intelligence and greater degree of freedom—is able at any given time to contribute more to the development of himself and his society than other creatures, the success of his building is dependent upon his use of the foundations which were laid by those who labored before him. The generation which has no regard for the accomplishments of former times will make no progress in its own time. If one would profitably exploit the possibilities of the present, he must first successfully appropriate the treasures of the past.

We are not saying that *everything* from the past must be built into the structures of the present. Carlyle overstated the case when he said that "the Present is the living sum-total of the *whole* Past."[1] To a certain extent the past does determine the kind of structures we can erect in the present. The foundation of our building is laid by the past, and as the Apostle Paul once pointed out to the early Corinthian Christians, "No other foundation can anyone lay than that which is laid" (I Corinthians 3:11). The *whole* building, however, does not have to be a duplicate of the buildings of the past. Within certain limitations, above the foundations, we can be selective in our use of materials from the past and creative in our own additions to them. George Santayana is right in saying that we cannot repudiate any one of our ancestors,[2] but we can decide for ourselves which ones we are going to emulate, and what our own personal contribution to the continuing family enterprise will be.

This is the point of perpetual tension in our understanding and use of history. Having accepted certain fixed foundations from the past as the base on which we must labor, how much of our building is to be a repetition of past experience, how much a readaptation of the past, and how much the work of our own creative imagination and effort? The first step toward a resolution of this problem is to accept, as Lord Byron did, the fact that

> ... History, with all her volumes vast,
> Hath but *one* page. . . .[3]

We must accept the unchangeable relatedness of life as it stretches in one long unbroken line through past, present, and future. We must then also accept responsibility for re-evaluating and re-deploying what life brings to us, and for making our own contribution to its on-going development. Whitehead reminds us that the running stream of life can purify itself in its onward flow, *or* lose its virtue along the way.[4] Whether life will tend to improve or deteriorate as it flows through our generation depends largely on the thoroughness of our appreciation of history and the integrity of our response to the challenge of the present.

This dependence of the present on the values of the past was something that was clearly understood by the people to whom the Fifth Commandment was given, and something to which they gave proper attention. While the Hebrews of the Old Testament period never produced what we might want to call a well-formed philosophy of history, they did have an acute sense of the continuity of life. From earliest times they laid great stress on the construction of the necessary bridges over which cultural values might be conveyed from one generation to the next. While the instruments fashioned for this purpose were sometimes physical memorials such as the stonework monument erected in commemoration of the entry into Canaan (Joshua 4:1-9), more often they took the form of myths, epics, customs, social institutions, cult practices, and compilations of moral and religious precepts. Circumcision, dietary habits, Sabbath observance, religious instruction, literature, and the Law—apart from their function in meeting other needs—served also to keep intact the tenuous lifeline which runs out of the fixed past into the fluid present. The whole of the book of Proverbs consists of nuggets of wisdom culled from the experiences of the past and presented as moral precepts and prudential maxims relevant to the continuing development of the race through succeeding generations.

It was in terms of this view of the continuity of life that we were able in our study of the Second Commandment to understand the reference made there to the effects which the sins of parents have on the lives of their children. It is in the light of this same concept of the historical relatedness of life that we can also best understand the accrual of value to children who honor their parents in those things for which honor is due.

ORDER AND GROWTH IN A DEMOCRATIC SOCIETY

The institution which had the most to do with order and growth in the Hebrew civilization of the Old Testament period was the family. As the social structure on which society depends most heavily for order and growth, the family is not peculiar to Hebrew culture. From the beginning of human history, wherever man has appeared, the family in some form has existed and persisted as that cultural institution which bears the basic responsibility for order and growth in society.

The fitness of the family structure and function is rooted in man's own nature, particularly the nature of his entry into this life, the nature of the process by which he reaches maturity, and the nature of the emotional attachments which are formed among those who are brought together by their mutual participation in these events. Man was brought into being as a result of the creative activity of God. In making man, however, God made him the kind of creature who could share with his Maker the responsibility for the full scope of his development as a person, including the creation of new human beings.

Every instance of human life appears as a result of the co-operation of two people—a man and a woman—in the experience of procreation, in harmony with the continuing creative activity of God. Thus the appearance of every new life necessarily brings together all the human elements essential to the formation and existence of a family—a father, a mother, and a child. This is the ultimate trinity of man. It takes its form and function from the God-given nature and necessities of man's own being, and upon its existence and proper functioning depend the orderly progress of the whole of human society.

Not only do the necessities surrounding man's entry into life bring the members of the family together; the necessities connected with the child's long period of dependence on other people tends also to keep them together. While the necessity of the father's co-operation in the basic experience of physical procreation is quite temporary, the partial dependence of the human mother on others for at least a part of the period of pregnancy and at childbirth, and the utter physical dependence of the child for such a long period after birth, call for some degree of continuing co-operation on the part of both parents. Since there is in the father as well as the mother a strong natural urge to see the ego perpetuated in the person of his offspring, the physical dependence of the child acts as a bond which tends to hold the family structure together.

In addition to these basic physical necessities, every instance of *human* life is surrounded also by social and spiritual necessities to which the parents are by no means irresponsive. Every human being—in order to be a human being—is a social being and a spiritual being, as well as a physical being. Social and spiritual qualities, therefore, are as much a part of the natural constitution of every *human* parent as physical qualities are. For this reason the natural urge of the parent to perpetuate the ego in the life of his child is a natural urge to perpetuate social and spiritual qualities as well as the mere physical aspects of life. This means that in order for the child to be well-formed at birth the atmosphere in which the mother moves during the months of pregnancy, particularly the immediate domestic atmosphere, must be one of security—especially emotional security—social harmony, and spiritual meaning. The being of the child, of course, is never fully formed at birth. His physical, social, and spiritual development to the point of maturity requires many years of continuous care and cultivation after he is born. This requirement coupled with the natural desire of both parents to keep the ego image alive in the child greatly strengthens and extends the natural forces which help to keep the family structure intact.

All of these reasons for making the family the focal point of our concern for order and growth in society were accentuated in the Hebrew culture of Old Testament times by the fact that it was practically the only institution able to provide any substantial help in meeting this particular social need. There was a primitive political structure and a burgeoning ecclesiastical organization, but neither of these institutions made any considerable contribution to the bringing of the child to physical, social, and spiritual maturity. There were no schools, no books, no child care experts, no Boy Scout or Girl Scout troops, no museums, no newspapers, no radios, no television sets, no art galleries, and no Sunday school classes. The transmission of the social and spiritual treasures of the past to a new generation was almost entirely the responsibility of the parents. Responsibility for the physical, social, and spiritual nurture and development of new lives was confined for the most part to the family.

While much of the task of transmitting accumulated cultural values and developing new personalities has been taken over by other institutions in our society, the family continues to be the basic and most important social structure in our civilization. The family must still bear the heaviest part of the responsibility for conserving and transmitting the values inherited from the past, for maintaining stability and order in society, and for bringing to maturity the kind of personalities which will make continued human progress possible. This is the insight of the Fifth Commandment. It sees the family structure and function as a permanent necessity of human nature and human progress and calls on each new generation to honor this indispensable relationship.

While the demand of the Fifth Commandment is addressed specifically to children, it has obvious implications for parents because the requirement it makes of children is not likely ever to be met unless the conditions necessary for such a response are imposed on the child long before he is capable of comprehending any kind of verbal instruction. One of the things which the injunction to honor one's parents surely implies is the subjection of one's self to duly constituted authority, but if there is to be any substantial hope that the child will ever respond satisfactorily to this demand, his parents must arbitrarily force him to conform to certain elementary patterns of behavior years before he can even be told that the Fifth Commandment exists. It is reported of Diogenes that on one occasion when he heard a youth swear he struck the young man's father. While this principle of parental responsibility for guiding the child arbitrarily into proper forms of behavior before he is capable of responding to reason, and for providing instruction and a proper example afterwards, should not be exaggerated to the point of relieving the child of his own responsibility, it also should not be neglected; for such neglect cannot fail to have a disastrous effect on the development of the child.

Basic among the things in which children are called upon to

honor their parents is—as we have just indicated—obedience. This is basic not only in the home but in all human relationships throughout life. During the nescience of early years the child's very survival frequently depends upon absolute obedience to parental authority. Subjection of the self to authority, however, is not an artificial human response which can be dropped after the early years of childhood. Subjection of the self to authority is a continuing condition of satisfactory growth and a meaningful existence. The subjection of the self to authority does no violence to the dignity of human personality and contradicts no principle of our democratic concept of life.

It is true that there are family patterns which are monarchical or otherwise dictatorial in character. The family system in ancient Israel placed a dangerously large degree of absolute power in the hands of the father. But while the absolute and completely arbitrary control of very small children by their parents is necessary, the continuation of an absolute and dictatorial rule is not the natural form or end of family government. The character and function of parental authority has its prototype in the Fatherhood of God. God is absolutely sovereign over all mankind, yet because of the kind of person he wants man to be—a person made in his own image, a person who possesses in large measure the same freedom of choice and action which he possesses, as well as a similar creative ability—he exercises his sovereign power and authority over man only to the extent that it is effective in bringing man to the maturity of self-discipline and a constructive use of his own creative powers. The authority of the human parent is to be understood as an authority delegated by God to one with whom he shares the responsibility of bringing a new personality to the maturity of self-discipline and creative self-expression. The obedience of the child to his parent, then, is not a craven denial of his own selfhood, but a normal and necessary part of the process of learning and self-development by which a full realization of all the potentialities of his nature may finally be experienced.

The child honors father and mother when he subjects himself to authority—their authority first, then other expressions of duly constituted authority in proper turn. It is important for us who live in a democracy to remind ourselves that this need for subjecting the self to authority is accentuated rather than eliminated by the democratic character of our society. The fact that we do not have one absolute dictator to whose authority we are forced to submit does not mean that we do not have to submit to any authority at all. It means rather that we must voluntarily submit ourselves to many authorities, and that on occasion we must exercise authority to which others are subject. Life under conditions of freedom—which is the kind of life human beings are intended to live—does not mean exemption of the individual from subjection to authority. It means voluntary subjection of the self to authority on the one hand, and the responsible exercise of authority on the other when it is our turn to play that role. The mechanic submits to the authority of the magistrate in matters of law; the magistrate submits to the authority of the mechanic when he takes his car to the garage for repairs. The physician submits to the authority of the policeman when he is driving on the highway; the policeman submits to the authority of the physician when he wants to have his blood pressure checked. The minister submits to the authority of the judge when he sits in court; the judge submits to the authority (spiritual leadership) of the minister when he goes to church. Such a mutual subjection to and exercise of authority is the indispensable basis of all order and progress in a democratic society.

The child honors his father and mother when he is amenable to instruction, not merely the instruction which he may receive from his parents but also that which he may receive from his teacher, his pastor, his Sunday school teacher, from books, and pictures, and good music, and museums, and nature, and experience in living, and from all history. This means that the child must be willing to devote himself to the self-discipline of study and learning, and to grow toward mature competency as a person through patient and persistent practice and drill in the arts and skills by which he is able to express himself and serve society at the optimum level.

The child honors father and mother when, having received and assimilated all that his parents have to offer him, all that history and heredity and contemporary culture have to offer him, he then accepts responsibility for himself, responsibility for providing for the physical, social, and emotional needs of his parents as they become decreasingly able to meet these needs themselves, and his proper share of responsibility for the whole society of which he is a part. The child does not honor father or mother by remaining ever a child, no matter how devoted he may continue to be to his parents. The aim and end of the family structure and function—including parental love, parental authority, parental example, parental instruction, and parental sacrifice—is to bring the child to the independence of maturity and to a mature acceptance of responsibility for himself and his society. When by obedience, amenability, and the acceptance of an increasingly heavy share of responsibility, the child prepares himself for and accepts this mature role in life, he honors his parents.

When by these means children generally prepare themselves for and accept this mature and responsible role in life, they help to make possible the fulfillment of the promise attached to the Fifth Commandment. This is a promise made not so much to individuals as to cultures and civilizations. In the Hebrew context of the Old Testament period it applied to the nation of Israel as a whole, not specifically to individual Israelites.[5] This promise does not refer to personal longevity, but to cultural survival. Its fulfillment is not to be thought of as a pat on the head for being a good boy, but the inevitable working of the natural law of cause and consequence. The Fifth Commandment states one of the basic conditions for cultural survival. The promise attached to it simply describes the result which inevitably follows when a people meet this condition. This is the character of all biblical promises and their fulfillment, just as it is the character of all natural law. In any case of natural law, such as the Fifth Commandment, the rewards of obedience are to be understood as being identical with the results of obedience. When children obediently assimilate the values brought to them from the past, conserve them, improve them, add to them, and pass them on as a sacred trust to the next generation, they obey the Fifth Commandment, and the result will be cultural survival and progress.

VI

THE SACREDNESS
OF LIFE

The most crucial problem men face today is their unfortunate habit of killing one another. This is not a new problem. The habit was formed in the infancy of the race, and people have been acting accordingly ever since. The problem is more acute today than ever before only because of the much more crowded conditions of the world at the present time, and because we now possess much more efficient and dangerous means of mass destruction than those which were available to former generations. If we continue the long-established practice of trying to settle our differences by killing one another as efficiently as our means permit, the early end of civilization is inevitable. We have at last reached the point of final and inescapable decision with regard to the practice of killing human beings as a means of solving human problems.

The solution to every human problem must be found within the nature of man's own being. There is nothing in human nature which suggests that killing human beings ever helps to solve human problems. The very essence of man's being as a human creature is the impulse to preserve and enrich the totality of life which he shares with all other men. This essential aspect of man's being is affirmed in the natural law which says "Thou shalt not kill." In our understanding of and obedience to this commandment lies the possibility that the human race may yet escape the violent destruction of itself which is now imminent.

The Nature of Human Life

There are those who believe that the injunction against killing contained in the Sixth Commandment applies to the lower animals as well as to man. The arguments of those who hold this view are not easily refuted. Certainly it is not sufficient to say that the natural law against killing does not apply to the lower animals simply because the particular religious writings in the context of which the Sixth Commandment has come to us contains other passages which seem to approve the killing of animals, at least under certain conditions. We have dropped and now condemn on the basis of a better understanding of natural (divine) law many inhumane practices which were approved, or at least tolerated, in these same writings. It is also not enough to say that as a matter of historical fact the Sixth Commandment actually refers only to the killing of human beings, although that is obviously the case. For while the legislation contained in the Decalogue, being an expression of natural law, is universally and eternally valid, these Ten Commandments do not claim to cover the whole field of moral concern. It is entirely possible that in time the continued taking of any form of animal life may be revealed to man to be morally wrong and totally unnecessary on any ground whatever. In this discussion we pass up any attempt to resolve this question, not because it is certain that the last word on the subject was given in the Decalogue, but because we can be reasonably sure that the Sixth Commandment itself does not forbid the killing of animals, and because we have at this time no knowledge of any other natural law which we understand to contain such a prohibition.

What the Sixth Commandment affirms is the absolute inviolability of *human* life. It is true that in its basic consistency the essential substance of the human body does not differ fundamentally from that of which the bodies of other animals consist. Biochemically, the physical life of man, like all animal life, is a dynamic organization of protoplasmic molecules animated by oxygen and oxidation. Physically, man differs from the other animals mainly in the greater manual dexterity which he possesses and in having a much more highly developed brain, by which he is able to reason efficiently and react to more subtle forms of stimuli with a deeper and wider range of emotional responses.

What puts man in a class vastly different from that of the other animals, however, is not merely his possession of a more highly developed physical body, but the fact that his being includes aspects other than the physical which other animals apparently do not share. Three aspects of man's nature are clearly discernible: the physical, the social, and the spiritual, all mystically combined to form a single living being—which we call a human personality.

There are gregarious tendencies in many of the lower animal groups which may be described properly as a kind of sociability, but such "socializing" differs most significantly from that experienced by man in that it has no considerable effect on the determination of the character of the animals which participate in it. There is, for example, no indication that one of these lower animals reared from birth in complete and permanent isolation from all others of its kind would ever be any different from one which grew to maturity in company with other members of the group. This means that while the lower animals may be closely associated physically, they do not appear to possess or to develop any cultural values, or consciously to communicate to their contemporaries or to the generations of their kind which follow them anything whatever which tends in any way to determine the nature of their being. Obviously, this is not the case with man. Man isolated from his cultural heritage and from the society of his contemporaries is inconceivable. To exist as a human being, man has to exist in, be shaped in part by, and participate in the shaping of, an environment consisting of the society of his contemporaries and the influences of the accumulated cultural heritage of which he and they are common beneficiaries.

The spiritual aspect of man's nature consists in an essential likeness to God which is the distinctive character of his being. This divine likeness in human nature is affirmed in Hebrew-Christian thought by the assertion that "God created man in his own image" (Genesis 1:27). This does not mean that God made man identically the same as himself in every respect, or equal to himself in any respect. It means that in making man God planted in his nature certain essential aspects of his own being not shared with other creatures. Man's spiritual nature consists in the moral character he shares with God, and in the possible continuation of his existence as a person indefinitely. To exist as such a moral being, man must be able to understand the will of God for his life, and be able to follow that will or not to follow it. In nontheological terms, this means that man is a conscious, thinking, communicative creature who is able to understand the nature of his own being, able to see the course he must follow in order to experience the fullest realization of all the potentialities of his being, free to follow this course or not to follow it, and responsible for his use of these capabilities or his failure to use them. Man partakes of the divine nature, therefore, in being intelligent, free, creative, partly self-creative, and morally responsible. It is in this respect, and to this extent, that he is a spiritual being.

There is no indication that this spiritual aspect of man's nature is shared in any way by any of the lower animals. To be dogmatic about this would be to deny the limited character of our human understanding. Certainly there are definite ways by which God is related to the lower forms of animal life as he is to all other forms of life. He is their Creator and the metaphysical ground of their existence. There is no discernible evidence, however, that the lower forms of animal life possess any of the spiritual qualities which would make the natural law, "Thou shalt not kill," apply to them in any sense in which it is applicable to human life.

In the fact that man is a social being and a spiritual being as well as a physical being we are able to see not only why the Sixth Commandment may apply to human life and not to other forms of animal life, but also why human life itself is to be considered inviolable. The Sixth Commandment is an injunction against the killing of the physical body of man, and we have seen that, basically, there is no difference between the physical life of the human body and the physical life of the body of any other animal. Why, then, is the killing of a physical human body a matter of any more consequence than the killing of the physical body of any other animal? As far as man knows, animal life other than that of man has no dimensions besides the physical which could be affected in any way by the decease of the body. The life of the physical human body, on the other hand, is so related to the social and the spiritual aspects of man's being that it cannot suffer being killed without seriously disrupting the life of the whole personality. This does not mean that the spiritual being of man—the spiritual values which may exist and grow and operate creatively and redemptively in an earthly, human personality—is ever destroyed as a consequence of the destruction of the physical body. It does mean that all the aspects of human personality are so inextricably interwined and tightly bound together in its earthly existence that the death of the physical body means the end of that precarious organization of physical, social, and spiritual forces which we commonly call a human being.

The spiritual aspect of man's nature—that part of his being which partakes of the divine nature—is the most meaningful part of human personality, and, like God, it is eternal. The physical body, however, is the concrete form or structure in which the human spirit plays its role in this earthly existence. By its very nature the physical body of man endures at best for only a relatively short period of time, but it is an integral part of man's nature to believe that the individual human spirit and the total stream of life can be significantly enriched by the increase of value which is possible during the manifestation of the spirit of man in a physical human body in interaction with other human spirits similarly situated. It is this universal human impulse to live and to enrich the self and the quality of all life by such living that the Sixth Commandment is designed to safeguard and encourage.

MURDER

The kind of killing which is universally recognized as a violation of the Sixth Commandment and almost universally condemned as being totally intolerable by any civilized society is what we commonly call murder. Murder is the premeditated act of taking another person's life, committed deliberately, and motivated by hate, envy, jealousy, covetousness (the desire to appropriate another person's possessions), the craving for a thrill, a hunger for attention, the desire to solve or simplify one's own problems, or sheer meanness. During 1959 one such murder was committed in the United States every hour.[1]

A murder rate as high as this poses a dangerous threat to the stability of any society. But more distressing than the actual number of these crimes is the moral callousness and strong inclination to violence on the part of people generally which these figures indicate. Because of the general condemnation of the act, and because the crime usually brings severe punishment to the guilty person, only a very small percentage of the cases of dissension, hatred, covetousness, conflict, and violence between individuals in private life ever end in an actual murder. For every case of homicide there are hundreds of less serious acts of violence and thousands of people involved in tragic experiences of hate, envy, jealousy, and covetousness. This disturbing fact is firmly established by the tremendous number of criminal assaults which are committed every year.[2] These less serious but much more numerous acts of violence indicate a dangerous prevalence of the emotional condition for murder in our society.

It is at this point that most of us need to discipline ourselves to resist the temptation to commit murder. Not many of us are constitutionally capable of actually taking another person's life. Most of us, however, succumb without any real resistance to the murderous emotions of hate, envy, jealousy, covetousness, and the desire for revenge. Jesus was aware of these acts of emotional homicide in human experience and branded them for what they really are. Conscious of the morally devastating effects which such uncharitable attitudes have on human character and human relations, he condemned them severely (Matthew 5:21-26). Speaking more specifically, but clearly in the spirit of the earlier example of Jesus, the author of I John declared plainly and without reservation that the person who hates another human being is morally as guilty of murder as the one who actually kills another person (I John 3:15).

Any successful attempt to reduce the homicide rate in our society must include a serious effort to eliminate the personal animosities, group prejudices, antisocial attitudes, and conflicts of interest which constitute the atmosphere of emotional tension in which the overt act of murder is always possible and probable if not actually inevitable. Such an effort must include a vastly expanded and modernized program of child education in the indispensable art of getting along with other people. Patterns of thought and behavior which have no place for physical or emotional violence must be made a part of every child's life at an early age by a process of instruction and training carried on in our churches, our schools, and our homes. Continuous programs of adult education in human relations and in emotional adjustment to ever-changing social conditions are essential to the maintenance of that emotional stability in individuals, families, and communities which is the only guarantee against the frequent occurrence of murder.

CRIMINAL CARELESSNESS

While the deliberate, positively motivated kind of killing which we have defined as murder usually gets the most public attention and calls down upon itself the severest condemnation, it is not the only or even the most common violation of the Sixth Commandment. An abundance of evidence points to the conclusion that in our complex modern society more people are killed as a result of carelessness than by the intentional and aggressive acts of those who are positively and maliciously motivated.[3] The crowded conditions under which we live in many areas and the high speeds at which we move about combine to make the loss of life as a result of carelessness a major problem of our times and a matter of grave concern to our generation. Our constant use of high-powered machines of various kinds places in the hands of those who operate them the power of life and death over all those with whom they come in contact. The safety of our lives depends a great part of every day on the sense of responsibility of those with whom we live and work. While the Decalogue itself prescribes no penalty for any violation of the Sixth Commandment, it is significant that the body of law in which this commandment appears provides the same punishment for carelessness which results in the loss of life that it does for murder (Exodus 21:12, 28-31).

One of the most tragic examples of criminal carelessness in our times is that which is apparent in the gruesome record of traffic fatalities in this country. More than thirty-five thousand people died on our highways in 1959. The number has not fallen below thirty-four thousand in ten years.[4] The total for the last fifteen years is greater than the number of battle deaths sustained by this country in all its major wars.[5] Sixty million Americans have been killed or injured on our highways since the automobile first came into use.[6] Not all of these deaths occurred, of course, in accidents which were caused by "criminal" carelessness. We do not accept the theory held by certain law enforcement agencies that there is no such thing as an "accident" which could not have been avoided. To hold this view is to deny the element of unpredictability which is always present in some degree in every life situation. We always live and act under certain given circumstances, some of which we can neither perfectly foreknow nor completely control. Because this is true, and because men are fallible and machines are imperfect and both are likely to remain so, *some* truly "accidental" deaths on our crowded streets and highways may be expected even when all possible precautions are taken by everyone concerned. But when an individual takes an automobile on the highway and deliberately disregards obvious and necessary rules of safety, or drives while intoxicated or otherwise incapacitated, and causes an accident in which a life is lost, he is clearly as guilty of a violation of the Sixth Commandment as the person who willfully and maliciously kills his neighbor with a gun. The proper regard for human life called for in this Commandment requires that we exert every effort to understand and control all the factors which may contribute to the occurrence of accidents in which lives may be lost or injuries sustained.

SUICIDE

A third violation of the Sixth Commandment which constitutes a very real threat to the stability of our society is suicide. The seriousness of the problem posed by this deliberate kind of self-inflicted destruction of human life may be seen in the statistics which show that suicide is very nearly two and a half times as prevalent in this country as murder.[7] The full impact of this tremendous number of killings is not felt by most people because suicides are seldom given as much publicity as murders or even accidental killings. The moral implications of suicide are quite similar to those of murder, but because it is self-inflicted and there is therefore no guilty person left to be hunted down, tried, and punished, everything connected with it is singularly undramatic, and consequently it is seldom given very wide news coverage.

Few of us are inclined to think of suicide as a crime at all. It tends to excite our sympathy rather than our censure because the perpetrator of the deed is also the victim of the crime. We are inclined to respond charitably toward suicide also out of a desire to be fair and helpful to the members of the family of the one who takes his own life. Certainly, it was a much to be desired step toward understanding, justice, and humaneness when society discontinued the vain, unreasoning effort to "punish" the suicide by outraging his dead body and confiscating his property. Obviously no one was punished by such barbarous practices except the innocent members of the suicide's family. It was a happy move in the right direction also when we dropped the insupportable theological dogma that a man's eternal destiny is determined and immutably fixed by the particular state of mind in which he happens to take leave of this life.

While the attitude of sympathetic understanding which most moderns have toward suicide is altogether commendable, it should not be allowed to blind us to the moral implications of the deed.

The charity which ought to be extended to the suicide and the members of his family should not be stretched to the point of condoning his action or encouraging others to follow his example. Suicide, under almost any circumstance, reveals moral weaknesses in individual personalities, and in the society in which it occurs, which are not helped in the least by glossing them over with a thin layer of cheap sentimentality. True charity will see that in almost every case suicide aggravates and augments rather than solves the moral and social problems of which it is symptomatic, and will use its influence not only to ameliorate the tragic effects of the deed but also to discourage the practice itself.

Nothing we may say on this subject should be allowed to obscure the fact that there is such a thing as a vicarious sacrifice of one's own life for others which is able to issue in a genuine increment of good and an increase of value for other individuals and for human life in general, which is in no case to be identified with suicide. Jesus and all the other great moralists have taught that a willingness thus to give the self for others is the ultimate expression of love. It ought to be remembered, however, that the need and therefore the possible efficacy and virtue of such a giving of one's life *in death* are contingent upon the presence and destructive activity of forces which are opposed to the good and which can be overcome for the benefit of any life only by the sacrifice of some life in opposition to them. This is the sense in which we speak of Jesus' death as being vicariously beneficial to all mankind. In order for him to overcome evil and encourage and help other men to win a similar victory, Jesus had to expose the evil of his day and oppose it with good, even though such a course of action was reasonably certain—under the circumstances which prevailed—to result in his being persecuted and ultimately executed. There is evil involved, of course, even in this kind of sacrifice of one's life, not in the sense that the one making the sacrifice of his life commits any act that is morally wrong but because the sacrifice is made necessary by the aggressive destructiveness of evil forces which are alien to and contrary to the nature of life itself.

Both reason and charity indicate that our approach to the

problem of suicide should be one which sees this deed as being contrary to the very nature of man and seeks earnestly to prevent it by making every effort to discover and correct the malformations of character and society which cause it. One authority on the subject gave what appears to be a valuable clue to at least one major cause of suicide when he said that "self-destruction comes about as a result of (apparently) insuperable difficulties in adjusting one's self to the complexities of environment."[8] This person has also suggested two quite familiar things which he believes to be essential and most effective in the effort to prevent the occurrence of suicide.

> Our intelligence and our affections are our most dependable bulwarks against self-destruction. To recognize such a force within us is the first step toward its control. To "know thyself" must mean to know the malignancy of one's instincts and to know as well one's own power to deflect it. . . .
>
> To the support of our intelligence we must bring the conscious and purposive direction and encouragement of love. In the function of friendship, that conventional term for the controlled investment of love, we must place the highest hopes. Both for those who would save themselves and for those who would save others, it remains our most powerful tool.[9]

CAPITAL PUNISHMENT

Another violation of the Sixth Commandment which lays a heavy burden on the civilized conscience of this generation is the now obsolete and inexcusable practice of capital punishment. This violation occurs when a society, acting "legally" through its courts and its law enforcement officers, "punishes" a person for some crime by taking his life. While there were two hundred offenses punishable by death in England as recently as 1807, capital punishment in most countries today is seldom imposed except for very serious crimes such as murder, rape, treason, and kidnaping.

The actual *number* of cases in which capital punishment is imposed is not particularly impressive when this figure is compared with those for other kinds of killing. The annual average for the United States during the decade of the fifties was seventy-four, a figure which is especially encouraging because it represents a significant decline in the frequency with which the death penalty has been imposed over a period of several decades.[10] The truly alarming thing is that *any* human life should be taken by society when such drastic action is not necessary to protect the public interest. The moral principle involved and violated when the state imposes the death penalty is the same whether it be imposed on one person or a thousand.

While the destruction of even one human life is never to be taken lightly, the really devastating thing about capital punishment is the guilt and moral distress which must be shared by every member of the society which permits it. Capital punishment, like all other legal punishments, is imposed by all the citizens of the state acting through their chosen representatives. Officials of the state who actually execute condemned criminals attempt to excuse themselves by saying that in doing so they act merely as agents of the people they serve with whom the whole of the responsibility for the deed rests. Such officials cannot justify their actions by such reasoning, but they are certainly right in implicating the other members of their society in the moral responsibility which they must share. In a democracy such as ours, government is the responsibility of all the people; and as long as capital punishment is practiced by the state, however seldom the death penalty may actually be imposed, we are all guilty of violating the Sixth Commandment, and all equally obligated to work for the elimination of this evil from our society.

We cannot lightly pass over the opinion of many responsible law enforcement officers that capital punishment is still a valuable and necessary deterrent to crime.[11] As keepers of the peace these men are faced with problems of tremendous proportions and almost unbelievable complexity. They are sincere men. They work hard at their jobs. They are entitled to the sympathetic understanding and whole-hearted co-operation of every citizen. The facts, however—such as they are—simply do not give substantial or unquestionable support to their opinion concerning the value and necessity of capital punishment as a deterrent to crime. There is no evidence that major crimes occur at a higher rate in the nine American states which do not practice capital punishment than in those which do. The crime rate in Michigan is not notably different from that in any other similar state, although they have had no capital punishment (except for treason) in a hundred and thirteen years. The dozens of countries which no longer practice capital punishment have no crime situations which differ significantly from those existing in the countries which do.[12] It is very likely that capital punishment does have *some* value as a deterrent to crime. The evidence now available, however, does not prove that capital punishment is *essential* to any modern society as a deterrent to crime, or that it is *any more valuable* as a deterrent to crime than imprisonment or other forms of discipline which are now possible and practicable.

While capital punishment in any case is a violation of the Sixth Commandment, at some points in history it may have been relatively justified on the ground of practical necessity. Under primitive or emergency conditions, where no attempt at rehabilitation could be made and no prolonged imprisonment was possible, where the execution of the incorrigibly criminal was the only alternative to letting them prey on the innocent without restraint, the practice of capital punishment was the less reprehensible of the two evils, and the one which every right thinking person was forced to choose.

We are faced with no such narrowly limited choice today. Present political and economic conditions make the humane imprisonment of those for whom such restraint is necessary universally practicable for any length of time. New medical information and techniques in testing enable us to know when a person of antisocial habits should be treated as a criminal and when he should be treated as a patient in a mental institution. Increased knowledge of psychology and new methods in psychiatric therapy make it possible for us to rehabilitate and restore to social responsibility many people whom society under different circumstances may have been forced to consign to the gallows.

Whatever may have been the case in former times, because of the more humane and socially constructive ways of dealing with this problem which are open to us capital punishment today is a denial of the redemptive power of God and an evasion of the redemptive responsibility of the human community.

Because society has a duty to protect its members from both the direct and the indirect effects of crime, as well as to deal humanely and redemptively with the criminally inclined, it is not enough simply to abolish capital punishment and concentrate on the humane restraint and possible rehabilitation of the criminal. All the resources of our economy, our educational facilities, our religion, and our social and medical sciences must be brought to bear on the development of strong personal character and socially acceptable habits on the part of all our citizens during their formative years. The best methods of dealing with the criminally errant will not solve the problem of crime unless society moves effectively to prevent crime by correcting those social conditions and practices which tend to develop the criminal personality and to make crime attractive and profitable.

WAR

The most serious violation of the Sixth Commandment is the destruction of human life which occurs in the course of international conflict. This is obviously true in terms of the number of people killed. There were over eight million battle deaths in World War I. There were more than sixteen million in World War II.[13] During and since the last great war nuclear weapons have been developed which are capable of total destruction. Now that the major countries on both sides of the world power struggle have such weapons, the complete destruction of human life must be viewed as a possible result of any future war.

The destruction of human life in international conflict is the most serious violation of the Sixth Commandment also because of the morally irresponsible attitude toward the taking of human life which usually prevails among a people at war with another country. While some attempt has been made to set up minimum international standards of humaneness for nations involved in violent conflict, killing as many of the enemy as possible by whatever means one may devise is generally considered to be a legitimate and necessary part of the grim business of war. Killing the citizens of an enemy country in time of war is commonly encouraged and sometimes even glorified by the very people who at all other times earnestly proclaim the sanctity and absolute inviolability of human life. Because of the methods and the kind of weapons that must be used in modern warfare, this license to kill is necessarily extended to include civilians as well as military personnel. Also, because of the vast amount of material resources needed to support the modern war effort, practically the whole population of a warring nation, civilians no less than the citizens in uniform, are directly or indirectly involved in the killing of their enemies.

It is frequently argued that the killing which occurs as an act of war lacks the moral stigma of other types of killing because the individual citizens of the warring countries are not motivated in their destruction of human life by hate for those they kill, but only by a sense of duty to their own country. This argument raises some questions worthy of consideration, but it is not valid in itself. For one thing, while the absence of hate from the human heart is commendable at all times, its absence as a motivating force in an act of killing does not necessarily justify homicide under any condition. If anything, killing in cold blood is more reprehensible than killing in hot blood. Furthermore, the prodigious official and unofficial effort which is always made when a country goes to war to arouse hate, contempt, and a desire for revenge on the part of its citizens against the citizens of the enemy country tends to make highly suspect any assumption that individuals are not motivated by hate when they take part in the slaughter of war. It must be admitted also that under no acceptable standard of morality does one's duty to his own country relieve him of his duty to be equally concerned about the well-being of human life everywhere.

While there can never be any absolute justification of war on the ground of patriotic duty alone, man's duty to protect and promote the well-being of all human life to the extent of his ability requires his co-operation in establishing and maintaining as much order and justice in the world as possible. Men and nations being what they are, the maintenance of such order and justice requires a use of force which may sometimes need to be carried to the point of killing human beings from whose injustice and violence innocent people can be protected by no other means. Such a use of force is essential to the maintenance of both domestic and international order. This is why absolute pacifism is not compatible with any realistic assumption of social responsibility. No human being or cause in this world is perfect. All people and all the ways of life they pursue are only relatively right or relatively wrong. Any decision we make as socially responsible people is at best only a choice between a relatively good and a relatively evil situation or course of action, although in the over-all determination of our decision we may be guided by a faithful and enlightened regard for absolute moral principles. This is the kind of choice which is forced upon us when the conflict of human interests at the international level reaches the point of violence. It is never a choice between absolute good and absolute evil. Even if the cause of one party to such a struggle were absolutely wrong (which is seldom the case) the choice would not be one between absolute good and absolute evil, because war—while it may be the best means we can use to sustain the right in a given situation, and therefore the means we must use—is never absolutely good. To protect and to support what appears to be good and right, even though it is only relatively good and right, against that which seems to be evil and wrong, even to the extent of war if necessary, is the personal and social responsibility of every man. No one, however, should be led by this grim necessity to forget that war itself is an evil which man must expend every possible effort to eliminate from human experience. We must maintain an uneasy conscience about war even when circumstances force us to use it to preserve —if only temporarily—that which is good. To the extent that demonstrations of absolute pacifism help to accomplish this, they undoubtedly have some value.

The most serious guilt we bear in connection with the continued use of war in the power struggle among the nations is our refusal to admit that war is an evil per se, our refusal to accept the fact that—whatever the case may have been in the past—war is now no longer inevitable, and our failure to work at the job of preventing war before the onward thrust of events which force it upon us is too great to be stopped. As the situation now exists, the sin of war is committed more in time of peace than during the actual period of violent conflict. They are more guilty who allow war to come by their apathy in peace than they who fight and kill when the conflict which is thrust upon them cannot be avoided.

There is happily some evidence that we may be awakening to our responsibility—not only to fight as bravely and effectively as possible when war is inevitable and the only means left whereby we may be able to preserve some part of what good there may be in our civilization—but also to exert ourselves energetically and resourcefully at all times in a continuing effort to make war unnecessary and improbable if not actually impossible. For some time our attitude toward war has been growing steadily more realistic. When Machiavelli published his eulogies in praise of the virtue of war in the early years of the fifteenth century they were generally accepted as fact.[14] Before the end of the nineteenth century William T. Sherman could say that "War . . . is . . . hell" with absolutely no fear of serious contradiction.[15] The sentiment which prevails most widely at the present time was expressed by Major General Smedley D. Butler when he said, "To Hell With War."[16]

No one should assume, however, that a general disposition to be done with war is enough to assure the world of a peaceful future. Peace is possible. It is not inevitable. Peace will not come of its own accord. The maintenance of permanent peace is a task which requires at least as much imagination and effort as the winning of a war. Recurrent war will give way to permanent peace only when men work for peace with the same courage, vigor, ingenuity, and perseverance with which they have traditionally waged war. A part of the task of peace is the formation of a new pattern of international relations in which war has no place. Precisely what this pattern will be like does not yet appear. There is no precedent for permanent peace. But one thing is sure. When it does appear, it will necessarily include a universal regard for the sacredness of life.

THE DIGNITY
OF PERSONALITY

The concern of the Seventh Commandment is for the dignity of personality. Adultery is forbidden because it violates that dignity. Adultery is a violation of the dignity of personality because it involves the use of one person by another as a mere means to an end. Such a use of personality is a two-edged sword. It destroys the person thus used *and* the person who so uses him.

The Nature of Personality

"Personality" is the comprehensive term we use to designate the totality of man's being as a psycho-socio-physical creature. Man has a physical body which is basically unlike that of other animals only in its superior capacities and in the superior development and use of those capacities. But totally unlike other animals, man is essentially spiritual in nature, which is to say that in common with God whose child he is, he possesses freedom of thought, decision, choice, and action, the capacity to know good and evil and the ability to accept or reject either the one or the other, and a quality of endurance which amounts to the possibility of eternal existence.

Mere physical birth alone does not endow any individual with what we call "personality." The physical organism of man does not become a human being by virtue of physical birth alone. This fact, now generally accepted by modern sociologists,[1] was recognized no less clearly by Jesus and was made the whole point

100

of his discussion with Nicodemus. "Unless one is born anew," Jesus insisted, "he cannot see the kingdom of God. . . . That which is born of the flesh is flesh, and that which is born of the Spirit is spirit" (John 3:3, 6).

Human personality does not spring into being as a result of the birth of the physical body alone. Personality—that is, *man* in the full sense of the word—comes into being only with the emergence of a spiritual consciousness—a "God-consciousness," to use Schleiermacher's term—on the part of the individual, and through the communication and interaction of this physically embodied spirit with other such spirits and with the Spirit of God. By means of heredity man is endowed at the birth of the physical body only with the capacities, potentialities, and limitations which make *possible,* but not *inevitable,* the development of personality—that is, the distinctively *human* aspects of his nature. Personality itself—man as a *human* being, as a true child of God, as a full-fledged citizen of the Kingdom of God—comes into being as a result of physical embodiment, *plus* the awakening of the essentially spiritual aspect of his nature, *plus* the social conditioning which comes about through his response to the limitations of an earthly environment and his association with other spirits—other men and God.

We may say, then—as we have said before—that man is a physical, a social, and a spiritual being. Personality, therefore, is the total and unified substance of a physical embodiment, a purposefully directed spiritual consciousness, and the relations which exist between one such being and others of a like or similar nature.

In our consideration of the sacredness of life as expressed in the Sixth Commandment, we discovered that the physical life of man is sacred and must be held inviolable from the moral point of view specifically because it is inextricably involved in the single complex pattern of human personality which is made sacred in its totality by its essentially spiritual nature—that is, by its God-likeness and by its continuing Father-child relationship with God. We have reviewed our concept of the nature of man at this point with special emphasis on the wide scope and varied aspects of that nature as comprehended in the idea of "personality" in order to show that *every* element in the being of man—even the less tangible social relations and emotional influences which we have seen to be equally real components of human personality—is equally sacred and that any violation of their sanctity is what the Seventh Commandment forbids.

The Sixth Commandment forbids the killing of the physical body of man because the physical body is an integral part of the total unified being of man, and because the dissolution of the body disrupts the total being and function of the human personality in its earthly manifestation. The Seventh Commandment calls attention to the fact that the total being of man can be corrupted, weakened, and destroyed as surely by violations of the sanctity of the nonphysical aspects of personality as by attacks on the physical body. This is an insight which has been shared by many of history's most honored sages. It has indeed been the virtue of most of them that they have seen the violations of the dignity of the nonphysical aspects of personality as the most deadly and dangerous of all. Jesus, for example, commenting on the relative seriousness of offenses against the physical and the nonphysical aspects of personality, said to his disciples: "Do not fear those who kill the body but cannot kill the soul; rather fear him who can destroy both soul and body in hell" (Matthew 10:28). "For what shall it profit a man," he asked in reference to the relative value and significance of the physical as over against the spiritual or nonphysical aspects of human life, "if he shall gain the whole world and lose his own soul?" (Mark 8:36, K.J.V.) As over against and supplementing the Sixth Commandment, which forbids the killing of the physical body of man, the Seventh Commandment forbids any attack on or misuse of any aspect of human personality, especially those of a nonphysical nature.

FUNDAMENTAL ASPECTS OF MARRIAGE

While an unmistakable and unqualified prohibition against the destruction, injury, misuse, or impairment of *any* aspect of man's being is implicit in the injunction of the Seventh Commandment, the specific violation of the structure and dignity of personality which it forbids is adultery. Adultery is a violation of human dignity because it is a perversion of one of the vital relations between human beings of which human personality partially consists.

The Hebrew word "*naaph,*" rendered "adultery" in our English translation of the Seventh Commandment, did not originally have any reference to a violation of the marriage relation. It meant what we still mean when we use the word "adulteration." Basically, it meant the mixing—or the result of the mixing— of a base substance with a pure substance. By the natural process of linguistic evolution, the word came to mean the perversion of good practices, or the mixing of base practices with pure practices. It was first used in this moral sense, not with reference to perverted sex relations, but to describe the perversion—or "adulteration"— of religious devotion by the practice of idolatry. The Hebrews' ancient relationship with God was a peculiar covenant relationship by the terms of which they were bound to give to God a certain kind of devotion which they were expressly forbidden to give to any other god. As required by the Covenant, the Hebrews' relationship with God was of such a nature that they could not enter into the same kind of relationship with any other god without "adulterating"—polluting, weakening—and ultimately destroying their relationship with the true God. The Covenant between the Hebrews and God recognized the fact that the very nature of God and the nature of man make it impossible for man to enter into positive and constructive relations with more than one god. In its first usage with a moral connotation the word "adultery" was employed to describe man's futile, self-defeating attempt to serve more than one God, or something other than God.

Basically, and apart from the various legal aspects of the question, adultery in family relations means exactly the same thing that it meant in terms of the Hebrew Covenant with God. Marriage is a covenant relationship by the terms of which the parties to it have certain privileges and duties with respect to each other which they do not have and cannot have with respect to anyone else. Marriage is the union of one man with one woman for the purposes of sex fulfillment, the procreation and nurture of children, and the completion of the basic development and expression of personality through intimate communication and interaction with another human being enough like himself (herself) to be congenial and sufficiently different to be enduringly attractive and stimulating to the point of exciting him (her) toward the fullest and richest possible realization and employment of his (her) potentialities as a person.

The validity of the marriage relationship does not rest on custom or any arbitrary fiat. No valid reason for any particular kind of relationship or behavior on the part of any being exists anywhere except in the nature of that being itself. The character of the marriage relationship as we have described it is determined by no authority other than the soverign power of the Creator who in making man and woman gave to them the kind of nature which cannot be completed and the kind of destiny which cannot be realized on any other terms in the area of full-fledged interaction between the sexes. The practice of monogamy—the participation in a given marriage relationship of only one man and one woman—does not rest on the strength of cultic regulation or the coercive influence of civil legislation. That part of the relations between the parties to a marriage union which makes it different from any other relationship is simply so personal and so intimate that it cannot possibly be shared by more than two people without polluting—"adulterating"—the relationship and injuring all the parties to it. Permanence in the marriage relationship is a desirable and possible objective only because the demand for it and the possibility of it are present in the nature of the parties to the relationship and in the nature of the relationship itself.

It was to the God-given nature of human beings themselves differentiated as men and women that Jesus himself referred those who sought to know whether or not there is any valid basis for the idea and practice of permanent, monogamous marriage. Speaking of the marriage relationship and the men and women who enter into it—and quoting in part from earlier Hebrew writings—he said: "But from the beginning of creation, 'God made

them male and female.' 'For this reason a man shall leave his
father and mother and be joined to his wife, and the two shall become one.' So they are no longer two but one. What therefore God
has joined together, let not man put asunder" (Mark 10:6-9). The
ideal of a permanent, monogamous marriage may not—most
likely will not—always be reached in relations between the sexes,
but in their striving toward it human beings can be encouraged by
the assurance that it is not beyond the pale of possibility. From
the beginning of the creation the need for and the possibility of
such a relationship has been present in the very nature of the
human creature. Men and women do not need to despair of
reaching an ideal which they are prepared by the nature of their
own being both to realize and to enjoy.

The nature of the human person demands not only a marriage
relationship which is not "adulterated" by either physical or
spiritual infidelity on the part of either party, but also a relationship between unmarried men and women which is free of any
act which injures or threatens to injure any aspect of the personality of either of the persons involved. Sexual promiscuity on the
part of single individuals, no less than that of married people,
violates the principle laid down in the Seventh Commandment
because such relationships are not characterized by the kind of
mutual respect and protection and enrichment which every personality owes to every other personality.

Promiscuous sex relations—both premarital and postmarital
—nearly always involve the use of one person by another as a
means to an end, a practice which does serious injury to both
personalities. Because it is the feminine personality in such relationships who is more often so used, the attempt has been made
to set up a "double standard" of sex morality in a vain effort to
justify the practice. According to this standard, promiscuous sex
relations are presumed to be permissible for "respectable" men,
but not for respectable women. The practice permitted by this
standard is unacceptable because it involves the use of certain
feminine personalities not as personalities but as mere means to
an end, and because it assumes that one person can injure another
person without being injured by the act himself. There is nothing

in the nature of the human person which gives anyone the right
to use another personality—masculine or feminine—as a mere
means to an end. There is nothing in the differences which dis-
tinguish men from women which gives to either any right
which the other does not also possess. By the very nature of their
being, human personalities—masculine and feminine—are essentially equal in dignity and worth, and equally entitled to treatment which is in accord with this fact.

MAKING THE MARRIAGE RELATION MEANINGFUL

Marriage *can* be mutually meaningful and profitable to those
who enter into it and to the society in which it exists. Marriage
does not *automatically* or *inevitably* bring meaning, stability, and
happiness to the individuals who participate in it or to the society
which encourages it. Marriage is not a miraculously operating
sacrament or leaven which works of its own accord to bring peace
and joy and fulfillment to those who merely take the marital
vows or to the society which simply records the taking of those
vows. Marriage is a *working* arrangement by the terms of which
it is *possible* for two people—one man and one woman—*striving*
together to experience a richer and fuller realization of all the
potentialities of their nature than they could ever experience
alone. The extent to which the marriage relationship adds to the
realization of human potentialities for good depends upon the
faith, the intelligence, the diligence, the love, the patience, and
the persistence with which the parties to it exert themselves in
the deliberate effort to make the relationship meaningful.
Marriage is not a miraculous mechanism which indiscriminately hands out lasting happiness to every couple who mumble
their way through the magic formula of an ancient liturgy.
Marriage is a job at which we must work from the first "I do"
until "death do us part," and the benefits which accrue to individuals and to society as a result of our participation in the
experience are in direct proportion to the industry with which we
apply ourselves to the task.

Actually, much of the work essential to a meaningful marriage experience must be done long before anybody stands up to say "I do." Successful marriages are made in the nursery, not before the altar. In the tremendous and absolutely indispensable task of preparing young people for a meaningful experience of marriage, every responsible institution in society must have a share: the home, the church, the school, and the state. Among these none is more important than the home. The young person's concept of marriage and his approach to it is determined to a greater extent by what he sees and hears and feels in the home than by any other influence. Fortunately, a great part of the preparation for marriage which the young person needs is provided by the general atmosphere of happiness and the normal process of spiritual nurture which prevail in every well-ordered family situation. This early development of a well-rounded personality in a happy family environment is considered by sociologists to be one of the most important factors in the experience of a meaningful marriage relationship.[2] What is needed in addition but seldom provided for children and young people in the home is explicit instruction and definite guidance in matters of sex, dating procedure, marriage, and the assumption of family responsibilities. While their own behavior as marriage partners is usually quite acceptable, most parents find it extremely hard to communicate verbally to their children the basic information about sex and family relations which they must have in order to make an intelligent approach to marriage. They commonly experience great difficulty in the effort to give to their children the practical guidance they need in making the decisions and forming the habits which are essential both to the experience of wholesome premarital boy-girl relations and to the ultimate experience of a meaningful marriage relationship. Acceptably effective skill in the performance of these basic duties which every parent owes to his child can be developed—and should be developed—through the study of some of the better books on the subject, conversation with experts in the field as well as with other concerned parents, and persistent practice.

The church can—and should—function effectively in the effort to make the marriage relation meaningful by making as clear as possible the theological and metaphysical facts on which the Hebrew-Christian concept and practice of marriage rests—that is, by keeping in proper focus the ultimate realities in terms of which any meaningful relation between the sexes, and any constructive family experience, must be patterned. The church can be helpful also in educating and training young people and parents in the principles and skills of meaningful relations between the sexes, both premarital social relations and marriage relations. One pastor preaches a series of sermons on marriage and the family at the beginning of each new year. Sunday school classes and youth forums can be used effectively for education in the moral and spiritual aspects of marriage. Serious and thorough premarital instruction should be given to all couples definitely planning to be married who will receive it, and required in the case of all those who wish to be married under the auspices of the church. The church should not attempt to exercise any coercive control over the marriage experiences of individuals, but it should insist that the moral and spiritual aspects of marriage be kept in proper perspective in any marriage experience in which it is expected to participate. The practice of some churches in denying to their members certain other ministries of the Christian fellowship as a penalty for their failure to conform in their marital practices to the official ecclesiastical opinion in such matters does not seem to be especially helpful to anyone, but the church should be careful not to allow itself to be maneuvered into any position which would imply approval of any marriage principle or practice which denies or disregards the moral and spiritual implications and responsibilities of marriage.

When one speaks of the "school" in this country, he is speaking for the most part about an institution and function of the state. For this reason, not too much can be expected in the way of education for marriage in the greater part of our school system, because many of our marriage principles and practices are considered to be synonymous with certain of our religious principles and practices, and the public schools here are prohibited by the constitution from teaching anything which might reasonably be interpreted as "religion." There are, however, many wide

areas of marriage experience—specifically the biological, the sociological, the economic, and the legal—which can be made the
subject of an intensive education effort in our public schools
without any serious danger of violating the constitution or the
sanctity of any individual conscience. Much is being done in
this field in our public schools now, and the effort should be
encouraged. Because this instruction is not under specifically
"religious" auspices, and because it does not deal with what are
commonly considered the distinctively "religious" aspects of
marriage, is no reason for alarm on the part of any religious
enthusiast, and no reason for its not being of great value to the
success and meaningfulness of the marriage relation. As Don
Martindale has appropriately pointed out, "The human family
is built about the very things man shares with all life: food,
growth (of the young), adaptation (of young and old), reproduction."[3] It is just as important to the success of the total marriage
experience that a young couple know how to balance a family
budget as it is that they be able to recite what the catechism of
their church says about the spiritual significance of the marital
union.

The interest and function of the state in connection with the
marriage relationship is related primarily to its concern for the
orderliness of society as a whole. The marriage relationship and
the family structure, which is its usual and fully developed
expression, is rightly recognized as the basic unit of society and
the one which touches more people more intimately and more
decisively than any other. It is therefore the concern and the
duty of the state to provide such legislation and such other aids
as are most likely to be of the greatest possible assistance in the
maintenance and regulation of the marriage relationship in keeping with the best interests of the individual participants and
society as a whole.

With regard to marriage the areas of direct concern to the
state are the qualifications for marriage, the solemnization and
certification of marriage, the relative legal status and rights of
husband and wife as such, the registration (of the birth) and
care of children and their legal status with regard to legitimacy

or illegitimacy, and the dissolution of marriage. One area in which the state might make a more substantial contribution to the stability and meaningfulness of marriage is that which has to do with the qualifications for marriage. In order to establish a significant social institution of any kind, those who propose such an undertaking must meet certain legal requirements laid down by the state to determine their qualifications for the establishment and operation of such an institution. The state gives some such attention to the qualifications of candidates for marriage, but those which are generally required at the present time are not broad enough to ensure an adequate degree of preparation for the responsibilities of marriage on the part of those who enter the wedded state. Requirements usually imposed in this country cover only such things as age, consent of parents in the case of minors, racial coincidence of bride and groom, proper certification, solemnization by a duly authorized person, a brief waiting period between date of application for marriage license and date of wedding, and minor health considerations. Obviously, all these requirements are merely routine regulations, mostly necessary and proper, but which provide no substantial encouragement, guidance, or assistance to the candidates in the decisions and preparations which are essential to a stable and meaningful marriage. If, as most of us are agreed, "the wedded state is earth's most sacred relation. . . . the very root of society, alike its basis and its bond,"[4] it would seem fitting that society should set the highest possible qualifications for marriage which are practicable, then do everything in its power to help the candidates for marriage measure up to them. In an advanced culture like ours it would not be unreasonable or in any way contrary to our basic democratic principles to make the entrance requirements to an institution so important as marriage include such essential things as a *thorough* medical examination, psychological and psychiatric tests, a minimum level of education—particularly in the areas of special preparation for marriage and family responsibilities, and vocational or professional training sufficient for reasonable assurance that the marriage and the family situation resulting from it would not normally become a problematic economic burden to society.

The emphasis in planning and applying such requirements for marriage would be not on excluding anyone *from* marriage but on preparing everyone *for* marriage. My thesis is that the need for and the possibility for a permanent, monogamous, meaningful, personally satisfying, and socially beneficial marriage relationship are inherent in human nature itself, and that such a marriage relationship can be experienced and will be experienced by normal people in a normal society if both the individuals and the society involved will exert a normal amount of energy to discover and adhere to the principles and practices on which such a relationship depends. What is needed is not more pious preachments about the desirability of meaningful marriage and the immorality of infidelity. The desire for such stability and meaning in marriage—desire in terms of an irrepressible need—is permanently built into the very nature of the human person. What normal people need—and what most of them will eagerly accept—is some practical help in making marriage work.

The concern of the state for the relative legal status and rights of husband and wife has been implemented quite satisfactorily in this country during the last century. Legislation in this field has firmly established the equal rights and privileges of husband and wife before the law and with respect to each other. The development of such a relationship of legal equality between husband and wife was in keeping with the democratic ideal of our constitution. It was also in keeping with the ideal demand of the Seventh Commandment. There is no doubt some validity in the opinion expressed by Conrad Moehlman that "the Seventh Commandment was addressed to adult Hebrew males" and that "its purpose was to protect the property of one male against infringement by another" because "the wife was the property of the husband."[5] It is certainly true that the social and legal status of Hebrew women in the time of Moses left much to be desired; but it is also true that their rights and dignity as human personalities were recognized and safeguarded by law and custom to an extent hardly equaled in any other culture of that day. While the property rights of husbands with respect to their wives as generally understood at the time may have received some temporary and incidental protection from the Seventh Commandment, its actual concern was for the dignity of personality, both masculine and feminine. Whatever its incidental effects may have been, the Seventh Commandment was intended to be—and proved to be— a tremendous step forward in the recognition and acceptance of the idea that the God-given dignity and rights of women are equal to those of men.

When we speak of the equal dignity of feminine personality, we mean simply that every woman, like every man, is to be treated as an end in herself—as a "person"—not as a means to some other end. That this was the dignity with which woman was endowed in her creation as a person, and that it was intended from the beginning that she be treated accordingly, are facts which were clearly indicated by Jesus in his discussion of this subject with his disciples. When they asked, "Is it lawful to divorce one's wife *for any cause?*" Jesus answered, "For your hardness of heart Moses allowed you to divorce your wives, but from the beginning it was not so" (Matthew 19:3, 8, italics mine). "From the beginning"—from and because of their creation as human beings—it was intended that women should be treated as God made them: equal with man in dignity and rights.

In the enactment and enforcement of legislation providing for and regulating the dissolution of the marriage relationship, the aim of the state should be to prevent such dissolution by means of reconciliation and rehabilitation whenever possible, to determine when a marriage relationship has deteriorated beyond the point of repair, and when that is the case to effect the divorce on terms best calculated to ensure the greatest possible degree of well-being for any children involved, to guarantee fair treatment with regard to property and other rights for both husband and wife, and to prevent as much disturbance and deterioration of society as possible. The most unsatisfactory aspects of the legal handling of divorce in this country at the present time are the lack of anything like a uniform law by which divorce proceedings are handled in all fifty states, and the general philosophy—or theology as the case may be—by which the legal grounds for divorce are determined. The first difficulty is a purely political problem which can and should be worked out by the states in co-operation with one another and possibly with the federal government.[6] The second problem arises out of a bad theology which has been implemented in terms of bad law.

Except in a few areas where marriages are dissolved with obvious irresponsibility as a kind of tourist attraction, the ground on which most divorces have to be granted, if they are granted at all, is adultery committed by one spouse as an offense against the other who is innocent and who must bring charges against the guilty party. This law works reasonably well in cases where these conditions actually exist—where one spouse is guilty of committing adultery against the other who is innocent. But there are any number of other reasons—spiritual reasons, psychological reasons, and sociological reasons—for the deterioration of marriages beyond the point of probable repair, and the truth of the matter is that most marriages that break down do so for one or more of these reasons rather than because of adultery. Because these more common reasons for the breakdown of marriage are not usually acceptable as grounds for a legal divorce, the result is that one party will actually commit adultery to provide a valid ground for divorce, or both will commit perjury in pretending that one has committed adultery, or they will simply separate and form other attachments without benefit of any legal sanction.[7] Certainly, no one of these courses of action is calculated to strengthen the moral character of individuals or to increase the stability of society as a whole.

One thing which would seem likely to improve this situation is for the state to recognize that the usefulness of a legal divorce lies not in the determination or punishment of the "guilty" party—even if there is one—in the breakdown of a marriage, but in the social and legal recognition of that breakdown and in the granting of a new legal status to the parties involved which will allow them to form other attachments and rebuild their lives as best they can in terms of socially approved customs and conventions. To suggest such an understanding and use of divorce is

not to abandon the ideal concept of marriage as being a permanent monogamous relationship. It is simply to recognize the fact
that failure does sometimes occur in the marriage relationship
and that the parties to such a failure should be accorded the
same understanding and help in reordering and rebuilding their
lives as are extended to those who fail in other endeavors. It is
to recognize the fact that divorce is not the *cause* of marriage
breakdown but the legal acknowledgment that such a breakdown
has already occurred and the legal clearing away of the debris in
order to facilitate the orderly and socially acceptable rebuilding
of the lives damaged by the debacle.[8]

Those who formulate and administer our divorce laws ought
to understand two things. They ought to realize that there are
possible causes for the breakdown of marriage other than adultery,
and they ought to understand that adultery itself is not *necessarily*
a cause for the breakdown of marriage, and that it therefore ought
not to be treated automatically as an adequate excuse for the
granting of a divorce. Every married person, as well as every
marriage counselor and every official who wrestles with the
problem of divorce, should understand that while there are many
attitudes and acts which *may* cause the breakdown of marriage,
no one of them is *necessarily* fatal to the marriage relationship,
and that therefore no one of them should be looked upon as being
per se a moral or legal justification for divorce. When Jesus said,
"whoever divorces his wife, *except for unchastity,* and marries
another, commits adultery" (Matthew 19:9, italics mine) , he did
not make some one particular sexual aberration an incontro-
vertible excuse for divorce as over against all other possible
violations of the physical and spiritual commitments of marriage.
If marriage works at all, it must work with the constant and
continued help of love, forgiveness, and redemptive self-giving.
There is no reason to believe that forgiveness and redemptive
love might not heal the hurt caused by adultery or "fornication,"
as effectively as they are able to deal with any other damage a
marriage might suffer. Certainly there are blows to the spirit
which are equally as devastating to the marriage relationship as
violations of physical commitments. If love, patience, and forgive-

ness can and should be applied redemptively in one case, surely they can and ought to be employed also in the other. Jesus must be understood as having laid down not a single particular *justification* for divorce but a high and noble principle for the guidance of married couples in the *preservation* of their marriages. Jesus was not interested in legitimizing even one *excuse* for divorce. He also had no interest in the perpetuation of any marriage relationship which violates the dignity of personality and mars the image of God in the human creature. He was interested only in the preservation and exaltation of that physical and spiritual union which enriches the lives of both parties to it and enables them to live in the bonds of matrimony more like children of God than they could in any other state.

The conditions for a meaningful experience of marriage have been stated nowhere more simply or accurately than by the author of Ephesians when he said: "Let each one of you love his wife as himself, and let the wife see that she respects her husband" (Ephesians 5:33). Mutual love and respect! Without these two ingredients no marriage can be successful. With them a marriage has a stubborn hold on life and meaning which is not easily shaken. In every relationship of life, but particularly in the marriage union, it is the giving of one's self that enriches personality and strengthens cherished ties, rather than the effort to get something for one's self alone.

VIII

THE RESPONSIBILITY
OF STEWARDSHIP

In 1903 Arthur Twining Hadley, President of Yale University, could see in the society of his day what he called the "signs of a demand for an increased recognition of the principle of trustee-ship in the handling of wealth."[1] Such a demand did exist in 1903 and has become ever more insistent during the years that have followed, but it did not have its origin in the beginning of the present century. It is at least as old as the Ten Commandments.

Precisely this—"an increased recognition of the principle of trusteeship in the handling of wealth"—is what the Eighth Commandment—"You shall not steal"—demands. In his possession and management of material things, as in every other aspect of his experience, man is a steward, or trustee, responsible to God for the use he makes of these values, and the appropriation by anyone of that which is committed in trust to another is strictly forbidden as being an interference with the exercise of his stewardship.

The Hebrew-Christian Concept of Property

In our American culture the most commonly accepted notion concerning the purpose of the Eighth Commandment is that it was given to safeguard the individual's right to the private owner-ship of property. A great part, although by no means all, of our American economy is based on the private ownership, control, and use of material things. Undoubtedly this particular economic

116

system, commonly called "capitalism," or "free enterprise," has contributed much to the material and spiritual well-being of those who live under it. It is quite natural and proper, therefore, that those who are committed to this system and benefit from it should use every valid argument to justify it and support it. It is altogether realistic to see in the Eighth Commandment a justification and safeguard of such a system of private ownership and use of property provided the "ownership" is understood as being limited and not absolute. When, as it frequently happens, the Eighth Commandment is interpreted as a guarantee of the right of man to the *absolute* ownership of property—private or collective—the meaning and intent of the Commandment are stretched beyond all legitimate bounds and twisted to serve purposes never intended by its author.

It is certainly clear that the Eighth Commandment is based on and is intended to safeguard *some* fundamental principle concerning the ownership and use of material values. We can understand and obey the specific commandment—"You shall not steal" —only when we are aware of and understand this basic principle upon which it rests. The principle underlying the Eighth Commandment does not establish man's right to the private ownership of property. It does not establish man's right to the collective ownership of property. It has nothing whatever to do with *man's* ownership of anything, private or collective. The Eighth Commandment itself has to do with a human right and a human responsibility, but this right and this responsibility must not be equated with the *ownership* of property. The principle which we are examining now does have to do with the ownership of property, but it is not *man's* ownership. It is *God's* ownership. The fundamental principle on which the Eighth Commandment is based is that *all property, as well as everything else, is owned by God alone.*

The principle of divine ownership of all property was well established in the Hebrew culture of Old Testament times.[2] In the garden of Eden story, none of the world's resources were deeded to man. He was simply given the privilege of cultivating the earth and making such use of its resources as is necessary to the fulfillment of his being. Ownership of the earth and all its resources was retained by their Creator, as a right belonging only to God. The author of the book of Exodus affirmed this common Hebrew understanding of the nature of property when he quoted God as saying, "All the earth is mine" (Exodus 19:5). The psalmist expressed the same opinion when he said: "The earth is the LORD's and the fulness thereof, the world and those who dwell therein" (Psalm 24:1). In what has been called "a perfect expression of the genuine Hebrew view of human property,"[3] the Old Testament concept of God's exclusive ownership of all things was clearly stated by King David as a part of a prayer of thanksgiving to God inspired by the generosity of the people in giving of their substance for the construction and decoration of a temple which was planned for Jerusalem. "Thine, O LORD, is the greatness, and the power, and the glory, and the victory, and the majesty," David declared, "for all that is in the heavens and in the earth is thine" (I Chronicles 29:11).

The doctrine of the exclusive divine ownership of all things is set forth in equally unequivocal terms in the New Testament.[4] Jesus' teaching leaves no place for the idea that man can have absolute possession of anything. In different but equally convincing ways both the parable of the Laborers in the Vineyard (Matthew 20:1-16) and the parable of the Rich Fool (Luke 12: 16-21) affirm the fact that man's "possessions" are only trusts and that absolute ownership belongs to God alone. That his disciples understood Jesus' teaching concerning property to mean that the things which a man holds are held as a trust and not as an absolute possession is clearly indicated in the Acts account of an emergency situation which arose in the experience of the early Christian community in Jerusalem. Describing the mutual sharing of resources with which these oppressed saints met and survived the crisis that was thrust upon them, the author of Acts said: "Now the company of those who believed were of one heart and soul, *and no one said that any of the things which he possessed was his own,* but they had everything in common" (Acts 4:32, italics mine).

This passage in the book of Acts provides us with unmistakable evidence that during one brief period of crisis a communal arrangement for the sharing of material resources existed among the believers in the early church at Jerusalem. It would be a grave mistake, however, to assume that this description of an isolated and very temporary practice of a purely emergency measure among one small group of early Christians constitutes an economic principle to be observed by everyone everywhere and at all times. There is to be found in this experience no directive as to which over-all economic structure is most in harmony with the Christian ethic. What this experience does make clear is the more basic principle concerning the ownership of property. According to this principle the ownership of all things is invested in God, and the property which any man holds, is held as a trust and not as an absolute possession.

THE BIBLICAL DOCTRINE OF RESPONSIBLE STEWARDSHIP

Man's stewardship relationship to God with respect to material things means simply that God owns everything, including man himself, and that anything man acquires, by whatever means, he holds not as absolute owner but as a steward or trustee, responsible to God for its use. The application of this stewardship principle may be seen in the ancient Hebrew law which provided for a Sabbatical year in which all debts were canceled and all slaves who had served for six years were freed (Deuteronomy 15:1-15). It is clearly evident also in the companion legislation which called for a jubilee, or Sabbath of Sabbaths, every fiftieth year during which every man who had lost his farm by any means whatever was privileged to return and take up possession of it (Leviticus 25:8-17). While these laws were difficult to apply in actual practice and many features of them were modified or rescinded by later Jewish legislation, the principle which they were designed to uphold is unmistakably clear: *God is the owner of all creation and whatever part of it man may hold at any time, he holds not as absolute owner but as responsible steward.*

While specific laws setting forth the stewardship character of man's relationship to his possessions such as we have cited in the Old Testament are not to be found in the New Testament, man's status as a responsible steward of all he possesses is made no less clear in the teachings of Jesus. Man's role as a steward responsible to God is revealed in the parable of the Pounds. In this story the nobleman—in whose role the person of God is portrayed—not only retains ownership of what he entrusts to the various ones of his servants, but also holds them strictly accountable for the use they make of his goods (Luke 19:11-27). This stewardship relationship is to be seen also in the parable of the Sheep and the Goats (Matthew 25:31-46), the parable of the Barren Fig Tree (Luke 13:6-9), and the parable of the Unjust Steward (Luke 16:1-12). Like Jesus, Paul saw man's relationship to God in terms of a stewardship which is not limited to, but which certainly includes, the responsible possession and use of material values (I Corinthians 4:1-2; II Corinthians 8:13-15; 9:6-14; Ephesians 4:28). With regard to the stewardship character of man's relationship to God in the handling of material things, the author of the book of James is explicit. He chides the merchants of his day for going about their business without regard for God's will in the matter (James 4:13-15) and confronts the responsible citizens of his community with the hypocrisy of their pious words of concern for the poor which are not backed up by any actual relief of their poverty (James 2:14-16).

In the light of the stewardship character of man's relationship to God, to society, and to the property he holds in trust, it is clear that the true intent of the Eighth Commandment—"You shall not steal"—is *to guarantee to man the privilege of responsible stewardship in the possession and use of material values.* At first glance the problem of stealing may seem to be irrelevant to man's practice of stewardship. If what a man possesses is not his own, if it belongs entirely to God, why should he be concerned at all about its being stolen? The answer to that question obviously lies in the fact that God has conferred on man not only the privilege of stewardship but also the *responsibility* of stewardship. Stealing would still be wrong, but the damage would not be felt so keenly by the victim if he were not accountable for that which is entrusted to him. God holds individuals and groups of individuals responsible for the care they take and the use they make of what he entrusts to them as stewards. If—as stewards of God—we are responsible to God for the use of that part of his property which he entrusts to us, our right to hold it and use it as stewards must be safeguarded against interference by anyone else. If God provides a man with a shovel for the purpose of digging a ditch, he is responsible to God for the performance of that task. But he cannot be held responsible for digging the ditch if his neighbor is allowed to run off with the shovel every time he puts it down. Stewardship implies responsibility. But there can be no responsible stewardship if the right to hold and use what God entrusts to one is not guaranteed. This is what the Eighth Commandment attempts to provide—*the guarantee that the stewardship privilege granted by God shall not be annulled by man.*

While a person's privileges and duties with regard to any property which he may hold must be understood and may be described most accurately as "stewardship," or "trusteeship," rather than "ownership," it can hardly be expected that the term "ownership" will be dropped from the vocabulary used to describe his relationship to the material things under his control. It would make for clarity and perhaps for a more realistic and wholesome attitude toward what are truly stewardship relationships if we did not use in connection with them this term with which the idea of absolute possession has become so inseparably associated. The important thing, however—whether we use the term "ownership," "stewardship," or "trusteeship"—is to remember that with regard to all our "possessions" we are actually only stewards, responsible to God who alone is the owner of all things.

Man's relationship to material things is to be understood in terms of his relationship to God. In the Christian faith the relationship which exists between God and man is described variously as that of Sovereign and subject, Master and servant, and Father and child. No matter what the analogy used to define this relationship, it always contains two characteristic elements: the sovereignty of the Creator and the responsibility of the creature.

It is in the light of this understanding of the divine-human relationship and the consequent stewardship relationship of man to
the material things entrusted to him that we are able to arrive
at a basic definition of the act of stealing. *Stealing is interference
with the stewardship of another by appropriating or removing
from his control any part of that which God has entrusted to him.*
To steal is to appropriate for ourselves, or to interfere with, anything which God has not entrusted to us.

THE PROBLEM OF STEALING
IN CONTEMPORARY PERSPECTIVE

At the time the Ten Commandments were given stealing was
a simple and easily recognized act. The culture in which the
Eighth Commandment first took its place was free of most of the
complications characteristic of modern society. Property con-
sisted mainly of land, houses, cattle, produce, a few farming tools,
clothes, household goods, and a very simple form of currency.
To commit an act of theft in those early days a person almost
always had to seize something concrete and carry it away with
him. An individual might accomplish a theft without being de-
tected, or complete a robbery without being apprehended, but
there was never any question about what constituted stealing.
The forms of theft were few and the techniques used were un-
complicated. Consequently, the simple injunction—"You shall
not steal"—could be given with reasonable assurance that everyone alike would understand what constituted a violation, and that
it would serve as an adequate and unmistakable condemnation of
every form of the crime which existed at that time.

No such assumption can be made with regard to the highly developed civilizations of today. We still have all the forms of stealing that were practiced in the days of Moses. These dishonest
practices are a nuisance and a threat to decent society now as
they have been in all the ages past. But as serious as these relatively simple and more obvious forms of theft are, they do not
represent the more dangerous part of the current problem of dishonesty. The more serious aspect of the problem as it confronts

us is that by far the greater part of the vast and intricate process of thievery that goes on continuously is never recognized or branded as stealing at all. The thievery that constitutes one of our greatest social problems at the present time is not the isolated act of pilfering on the part of some social outcast. The really significant and dangerous part of this problem is created by substantial citizens who occupy positions of prestige and power in the community and are considered generally to be quite respectable individuals. These people are not always—indeed, they are seldom—professional thieves, racketeers, or gangsters. Such disreputable persons—far too many of them—do exist and operate in our society. The greater part of the stealing that goes on today, however, is done by those engaged in some "legitimate" enterprise.

The widespread incidence of stealing in our times does not necessarily mean that the basic tendency of people toward dishonesty is any stronger today than it has been at other times. The unusually common occurrence of this crime in our generation is due to a combination of several factors inherent in the character of modern civilization itself. For one thing, material wealth today is represented more frequently and on a much wider scale by some medium of exchange or intangible form of value than at any other time. This means more than the mere fact that the use of money is more common today than in earlier periods. Stocks, bonds, shares, insurance policies, social security provisions, political patronage, and the influence of office or position are the things which figure more prominantly in our everyday economic transactions than such concrete commodities as cattle and tools and actual cash money. Such intangible forms of economic value lend themselves to a type of stealing at once more easily accomplished by those skilled in the use of this modern economic machinery and more difficult to detect.

Another factor which helps to account for the high incidence of theft in modern society is the size and intricate organization of our economic institutions. The complex system of ownership and management of our mammoth corporations tends to put the human relations involved on an impersonal basis that greatly lessens the concern for personal integrity. In such a system, in which each participant understands and performs only one small part of the total function of the organization, the individuals involved tend to feel no compelling amount of responsibility for what the corporation does as a whole. This tendency toward complex organization and impersonal relations in business is by no means limited to the large corporation. The modern organization and methods of even our smaller businesses tend to depersonalize the relationship between the individuals involved and consequently to obscure the question of moral responsibility. Obviously, when a business organization of any kind engages in a dishonest practice, some person or group of persons is no less guilty of stealing than an individual is when he commits the same crime acting alone. It is simply a fact of human experience that the more impersonal and complex human relations become, the less sensitive people tend to be to the propriety of their actions, and the easier it is for those who would deliberately defraud others to be dishonest and to cover up their guilt.

A third factor in the present situation which has made stealing one of our gravest current problems is the lack of clarity in our thinking with regard to what actually constitutes an act of theft. This moral uncertainty is a natural result of the revolutionary and far-reaching social and economic changes to which we have just referred. When the Eighth Commandment was first enunciated, economic structures were simple and the human relations involved were personal. Under such conditions, any violation of this Commandment was immediately obvious to the guilty person and to the society of which he was a part. That is not the case today. So complex is the economic system under which we now live that it is frequently extremely difficult to decide when an act of theft actually has been committed and even more difficult in many instances to determine exactly who has committed it. Many people on pensions and fixed incomes are convinced, for example, that they have been defrauded when their purchasing power is cut in half by the inflation of our currency. Are they right? If they are right, someone is guilty of stealing. Inflation does not just happen. Someone is responsible. But who? No one has yet answered these or any one of a number of other morally significant questions which have grown out of the economic practices peculiar to our times.

This does not mean that the Eighth Commandment is irrelevant to the economic system that exists today. It simply means that this Commandment has to be reinterpreted and reapplied in terms of existing economic conditions. Work on this continuing task of reinterpretation and reapplication has not been kept up to date. There is a serious lag between the development of our modern social structures and our interpretation and application of the Eighth Commandment in the light of the changed economic conditions which have resulted from it. Since the beginning of the industrial revolution, the previous understanding and application of the Eighth Commandment have been increasingly inadequate to meet the needs created by the rapidly changing character of our economy. During this time we have not done nearly enough toward rethinking the principle contained in this Commandment and making it applicable to the economic conditions that have been constantly evolving. This thinking must be done. The moral maturity of our generation, and, consequently, the well-being of our civilization, depend upon it.

Two things may be cited as being most responsible for our failure to do the thinking essential to any sincere effort to understand and obey the Eighth Commandment as it applies to the conditions under which we live today. One of these is that some people simply prefer a situation that is morally ambiguous. Such a condition allows them to claim for themselves the benefit of the doubt in any close decision between right and wrong. They can subscribe to the Eighth Commandment in general and disregard it in every particular instance in which it is to their advantage to do so with much less chance of being suspected or condemned by the society in which they operate. Such an arrangement allows them to maintain their piety and their dishonest practices with very little danger that the two will ever come into serious conflict.

A less obvious but perhaps more serious hindrance to the rethinking of this Commandment is the sheer intellectual laziness which has afflicted the modern world in the area of moral concern. From its beginning the industrial revolution has been

marked by an extreme activism aimed at changing the whole face
of the physical world. This does not mean that modern industry
has not employed intellectual as well as physical powers in working the technological miracles of the last two centuries. The capabilities of human reason have been exploited to the utmost and
with great benefit to all mankind in the development of the
physical sciences. The work of the human mind is never complete,
however, until it reaches beyond its victories over the physical
universe and properly relates those triumphs to the meaning of
the whole of life. That we have never done. The modern mind
always gets tired and quits before its job is completed. We think
our problems out with amazing clarity and effectiveness through
all the physical stages of discovery, design, and production. But
when we are confronted with the task of thinking through the
problem of making the technological genii we have created serve
the moral and spiritual as well as the physical needs of all mankind, we give up before we begin, exhausted and utterly confused.
Modern man's ability to think through his physical problems
more readily than his moral problems is another indication that
he is more a child of the humanism of the Renaissance than of
the religion of the Reformation. We are still trying to make God
superfluous in the universe, as the humanists taught that he is,
rather than the center of the universe, as the Reformers presented
him. While humanism has more or less successfully resisted the
less attractive influences of religion, the reverse is unfortunately
not true. Humanism very quickly entered the mainstream of
Reformation thought, with the result that in far too many instances professing Christians have had little more appreciation of
God as the sole principle by which all life must be understood
and ordered than their humanist neighbors. As Christians we
have not denied God, as the humanists have; we have simply
ignored him. The result, of course, is the same—except that the
humanist is not guilty of the hypocrisy practiced by the Christian
who professes allegiance to God as the sovereign Ruler of the
universe, then disregards his will entirely in all the practical
affairs of life.

THE MODERN PRACTICE OF THEFT

Purse-snatching, burglary, armed robbery, embezzlement, and blackmail are ancient forms of theft which are still practiced on much too large a scale in modern society. 1,921,537 burglaries, robberies, and other thefts were reported in this country during 1959. The value of property stolen during this period amounted to more than one half billion dollars.[5] These forms of theft are a great nuisance, but they do not represent the most dangerous aspects of the threat which stealing poses for the moral and economic stability of our society. It is relatively easy to keep these forms of theft under control because they are recognized by almost everyone for what they really are, and public opinion is practically unanimous in its condemnation of these practices. As bothersome and costly as these crimes are, it is nonetheless reasonable to assume that police surveillance, legal prosecution, and public opinion working together will prevent them from becoming a serious threat to our civilization.

Unfortunately, there are other forms of stealing, much more prevalent in our times, against which these restraining influences are not nearly so effectively arrayed. Many forms of stealing have been given the stamp of legal approval by state or national lawmaking bodies. Where this has happened police interference and legal prosecution of offenders have been made impossible, and public opinion has been confused and divided. In other cases, the law regarding certain types of theft is so ambiguous, or so lax, or so full of loopholes, that it frequently works to the advantage of the offender rather than as an effective instrument by which he can be restrained. It is in this broad, ill-defined area of dishonest dealings that the really dangerous threat to our society is to be found. It is here that the conscience of our civilization is most likely to be corroded completely away. Here we have a condition which is all the more dangerous because it is not obvious. A necessary part of any realistic effort to eliminate the practice of theft from our society, therefore, is the recognition and branding of these less obvious forms of stealing for what they really are.

One of the largest categories in the whole catalogue of modern theft is fraud. In the context of our present concern fraud may be defined as the appropriation of that which is the stewardship responsibility of another by means of deceit or trickery. By its very nature, therefore, stealing by fraud is among the forms of theft most difficult to determine and detect. Included in this category are all the practices by which money is received for goods or services which are represented and sold as having a greater or a different value than that which they actually possess. There are laws prohibiting the misrepresentation of goods offered for sale, of course, but the general lack of moral sensitivity with regard to honesty in trade makes it extremely difficult to exercise an effective legal control over this widespread form of thievery. Our pure food and drug laws, for example, have helped some, but the extent to which this fraudulent taking of profits is practiced in open defiance of both law and the commonly accepted principle of honesty is a scandalous and serious threat to both the moral and economic structures of our society.[6]

The foundation on which much of this subtle, insidious sort of thievery rests is false advertising. The basic purpose of advertising is to keep potential buyers informed as to what products are available and to provide for them a factual description of those products and their uses. Insofar as advertising serves this purpose it is beneficial to both buyer and seller. Advertising ceases to be a useful business procedure, however, and becomes an important factor in the practice of theft when persuading the customer to buy becomes its only aim, and when in serving this purpose it loses all regard for truth in the description of the product being offered for sale.

Along with transactions in which money is received as a result of goods being represented as having a higher or different value than that which they actually possess, we need to recognize as stealing also the practice of selling, by the same fraudulent method, products which are actually harmful to the buyer. This kind of stealing may be seen in the sale of narcotics for nonmedical use, and in the tremendous volume of business done by the alcoholic beverage industries. Of course, the claim is made by these industries that their product is beneficial to its users. It is indeed this very claim, which cannot be substantiated by the facts, which makes this ten billion dollar a year business in America[7] one of the most colossal stealing operations in our whole society.

We must label as stealing also the taking of money or anything of value as a result of any kind of gambling enterprise. It is often argued that since both parties to a gambling game enter into the transaction voluntarily no theft or improper action of any kind is involved. It is true that the person who loses in a gambling game participates in the activity voluntarily and with the hope that he will himself get something for nothing. This fact, however, does not prove that "winning" in a gambling game is not stealing. It simply proves that every participant in a gambling enterprise is equally guilty of stealing, or an attempt to steal, because it is the intent and effort of each alike to gain something at the expense of the other. The aim of each participant is to get something from the other which he is not willing to bestow as a gift and for which he receives nothing of value in return. It is estimated that at least fifteen billion dollars is taken annually from the American public by professional gambling interests.[8] This money is stolen, and those who are the losers in the "game" are as guilty as those who win. We can pity these losers because of their losses, but we cannot absolve them from the equal guilt they must bear along with those who take their money. Many of these losers—if not the usual winners—are among the most respected people in our country. This respectibility, however, does not alter the fact that their participation in a gambling game makes them guilty of fostering one of the most widespread and vicious forms of organized stealing with which our society has to cope. And the fact that many state governments have legalized this form of stealing makes their actions nonetheless reprehensible. We do not make stealing any less stealing by putting a legal stamp on it.

Another form of stealing which threatens the stability and strength of our society is that which occurs as an imbalance between wages and the work for which the wage is paid. An employer steals from his employee when he pays him less for his work than it is actually worth. An employee steals from his employer when the work he does is less than that which may rightfully be expected in return for the wages he receives.[9] Until relatively recent times, when an unjust imbalance between wages and work occurred, the offender was nearly always the employer. This was true not because employers were inclined generally to be more unfair than employees but because with regard to the fixing of the terms of employment the employer was usually in a much better bargaining position than the employee. Indeed, in most cases the economic strength of the employer was so much greater than that of the employee, that the latter virtually had no voice in the matter at all. With the rise of the labor movement the collective bargaining power of employees has tended to equal if not exceed that of the employers, and under these conditions the balance between wages and work is as likely to be upset in one direction as another. Powerful unions in existence today are sometimes able to demand and get wages and other benefits for their members which are worth much more than the services which are given in exchange.[10] When this happens it is no less stealing than when an employer who has the power to fix the wages of his employees pays them less than their services are worth. The complex and ever-changing character of our economy makes it impossible to devise any simple or final formula for the determination of what is a fair remuneration for a given amount of work. In spite of the fact that it is subject to abuse by either side, the process of responsible collective bargaining appears to be the procedure which at the present time is most likely to issue in a fair adjustment of wages to work.

The use of market conditions or the maneuvering of the processes of production and marketing in order to sell goods or services at a price which is unfair to individual buyers and incompatible with the permanent well-being of the total community is a practice that must be branded as stealing. The same thing is true also of buying goods and services. Any practice on the part of a buyer or combination of buyers which deprives the producer and marketer of a fair price for their goods is stealing. This much-involved question of fair prices paid and received takes us far into the complexities of modern commerce where no single, simple formula will serve as a detailed and permanent guide to justice and fairness in every one of the different and almost innumerable trade relations that exist in contemporary society. One of the most commonly quoted principles of trade on which the modern system of privately owned and operated capitalism allegedly rests is that in a free market in which the law of supply and demand is allowed to operate without restriction, prices will automatically rise or fall to that level which is fair and in the best interests of all concerned. As the best means of protecting consumers from the predatory trade practices of greedy and irresponsible merchants who by devious business maneuvers gain control of the market in many of the basic necessities of life and sell these goods for exorbitant prices, Martin Luther advocated a fair price ceiling on all essential commodities to be fixed and enforced by government.[11] Experiments with these two quite different economic theories indicate that some use of both principles is needed in most situations to help create the kind of economic environment in which the practice of genuine honesty and fairness in trade is most likely to occur.

Unfair evasion of one's just share of the common and necessary tax burden is stealing. Tax evasion is perhaps the most serious kind of stealing in America today, both with regard to the amount of the theft and the number of people involved. It has been reliably estimated that if every corporation, business firm, and individual in America would make an absolutely honest tax return every year, the entire national debt could be paid off in five years.[12] Testimony before the House Ways and Means Committee has indicated that self-employed persons on the average have been reporting only about seventy-five percent of their income for tax purposes.[13] Too many people seem to feel that stealing is not stealing if the victim of the theft is a whole society of people instead of an individual. One is no less guilty of stealing when he keeps for his own use what he owes to another than when he takes for himself that which belongs to another, and this is true whether that which is owed and kept for one's own use is owed to an individual or a nation.

IX

THE SANCTITY
OF TRUTH

The Ninth Commandment—"You shall not bear false witness against your neighbor"—affirms the social aspect of man's being. To speak of a man as a social being is to call attention to the fact that man can exist as a human creature only as he exists in relation to other men.[1] These relationships among men upon which man's humanity is partially dependent are possible only to the extent that the witness men bear concerning the reality of things is a true one. Every deception among men weakens the structure of human society in which the being of man partly consists. This kind of sabotage of the community of man is what the Ninth Commandment expressly forbids.

THE CHARACTER OF TRUTH

To the extent that it represents a sincere interest in the nature of truth, it is fitting that we reiterate and attempt to answer Pilate's famous question as a basis for our consideration of the problem of false witness. False witness is a misrepresentation of reality, commonly known as lying. As a misrepresentation of reality, lying is always opposed to truth. Some understanding of truth will be useful, therefore, in our effort to get the problem of lying in proper focus.

Pilate's curt "What is truth?" (John 18:38) may have been a cynical expression of disbelief in the existence of any absolute good, or perhaps an agnostic's sarcastic repudiation of the idea

that man can have any considerable or practically useful com-
prehension of such an absolute good even if it does exist. On the
other hand, it may have been an indication of the caution which
he felt should be exercised in accepting the absoluteness of any
humanly conceived and expressed standard of right and wrong.
Insofar as Pilate's question reflected a reluctance to accept any
example of human virtue as being an absolute good, it was sure
to receive from Jesus a sympathetic response. Jesus himself was
extremely careful not to confuse the absolute good with any
human manifestation of good—even his own. When a certain
important official addressed him as "good" Master, Jesus made a
point of inquiring into the sense in which the word "good" was
being used. "Why do you call me good? No one is good but God
alone" (Luke 18:19).

It will help our understanding if we can remember that this
distinction between the absolute and any and all of the partial
reflections of the absolute in human experience must be made
with regard to truth as well as goodness. Indeed, in the ultimate
sense—as absolutes—truth and goodness are the same. Absolute
goodness is the rightness of things in their tendency to create and
maintain valuable and value-producing structures and relations.
Absolute good is the Ultimate Reality by which the universe is
ordered, the Source and Ground of all that is good and constructively meaningful. Obviously, this is also what absolute
truth is. Absolute truth is the essential creative Substance of the
universe in its moral expression. This is what Washington
Gladden meant when he said

. . . that Truth and Right
Have the universe on their side.[2]

It was truth in this absolute sense that Plato identified as the
eternal ideas—or forms—of pure thought.[3] The idea of a
Creative Principle of Right which is at once the Source of all
good and the Substance of that cohesive orderliness which holds
the universe together was expressed by the psalmist when he said,
"Faithfulness will spring up from the ground, and righteousness

will look down from the sky. Yea, the LORD will give what is good" (Psalm 85:11-12).

The psalmist's identification of God as both the Source and Substance of absolute truth—truth as the eternal form and ultimate rightness by which all things are shaped and ordered—is not unique. A common conclusion of ancient Egyptian thought was that "God is the truth."[4] In New Testament thought the third person of the Trinity is described as "the Spirit of truth, who proceeds from the Father" (John 15:26). Jesus, speaking in his role as the Christ, the Logos, the human embodiment of the divine essence, said, "I am the . . . truth" (John 14:6). While it is altogether in keeping with the facts to say that God *is* truth, the character and power of ultimate truth are brought to bear on the various aspects of the universe for the most part in terms of the working of natural laws ordained by God. This truth character— and truth-serving character—of natural law was put in proper perspective by the psalmist when he said in a song of praise to God: "Thy *law* is truth."[5]

The word "truth" is used in another sense to indicate a coincidence between what a thing actually is and what it appears to be in human experience. This is the sense in which Whitehead uses the word when he defines truth as a "conformation of Appearance to Reality."[6] We say that a picture possesses the quality of truth if it faithfully depicts the scene or idea it is intended to represent. It is in this sense that the question of truth—truth understood as a correspondence between appearance and reality—is relevant to all human concepts. Man experiences concrete reality in terms of a set of sense perceptions and impressions. What a thing appears to be to man is determined by the character of these sense perceptions and impressions and the kind of intellectual interpretation and organization which he gives to them. The concept—the intellectually interpreted and organized sense-image —of a particular thing which a person has possesses the quality of truth if it corresponds to the reality of the thing itself.

The word "truth" is used in still another sense to indicate the factual accuracy of a verbal account, report, or description of an experience, an idea, a person, or a thing. In this use of the word, truth means "fact-reporting," or "truth-*telling*." This is the kind of truth which is called for in the Commandment which says "You shall not bear false witness against your neighbor."

Truth-telling is commanded because truth is the principle on which the universe is structured and by which it is sustained and ordered, and because any departure from this principle in verbal human communications is a denial of the truth-ground of all being, and tends to cut man off from the vital truth-forces in the universe upon which his existence and his well-being are dependent. Russell W. Davenport was brought to a realization of this fact in his search for a ground on which to base our hope and struggle for freedom.

> The possibility of real freedom exists, we may say, only where men enter upon a relationship to the universe around them. This relationship is not the result of academic philosophizing; it is brought about through the search for truth. The moment men begin to search for the truth about any situation or problem or circumstance, they create a relationship, however microscopic, between themselves and the surrounding world; and it is in this relationship that freedom becomes *possible*.[7]

Truth-telling is demanded by the very nature of man's being. In answer to the question, "Why am I bound to speak the truth?" James H. Thornwell said: "Because it is the law of my nature; it is a fundamental datum of conscience; a command of God impressed upon the moral structure of the soul."[8] False witness corrodes away the moral structure of individual being and tends to make impossible that interaction among individuals on which man's very being as a human creature partly depends. This is what Emerson meant when he said that "every violation of truth is not only a kind of suicide in the liar, but a stab at the health of human society."[9]

THE PROBLEM OF DECEIT

According to Mark Twain's computation there are 869 different forms of lying.[10] We cannot be sure about the accuracy of this count. It is quite obvious, however, that too many ways of lying have been devised, and that there are too many people using them.

The particular form of lying against which the Ninth Commandment aims its prohibition is perjury—specifically, the giving of false testimony against another person who is being tried in a court of law. While cases in their early history can be cited in which the guilt of individuals was decided by lot or magical religious rites,[11] the usual approach to justice among the ancient Hebrews was uniquely realistic. In Hebrew jurisprudence God figured as both the author and the final arbiter of the law by which justice was administered (Deuteronomy 1:17; 28:1-20; Isaiah 33:22). At a very early period, however, the people themselves were brought into active and responsible participation in the administration of the legal system by which the guilt or innocence of individuals was decided and the guilty parties punished (Exodus 18:13-26). There were no juries, although the function of "the elders" in hearing matters of civil law and custom as they sat "in the gate" was quite similar to modern jury duty (Ruth 4:1-12; Psalm 69:12). For the most part the administration of justice was in the hands of judges and witnesses. A high standard of integrity was required of the judges (Deuteronomy 1:16-17; 16:18-20; 25:1), and any defection from it was severely condemned (Deuteronomy 27:25; Isaiah 1:23-27; 5:22-24; Amos 5:11-24). Circumstantial evidence was not admissable as a sufficient ground for conviction. A person could be convicted of a serious crime only on the basis of testimony given by witnesses.

The fact that persons accused and tried before a court of law were convicted or acquitted largely on the strength of evidence given by witnesses made it imperative that all possible precautions be taken to prevent the giving of false testimony. This was one of the purposes of the Ninth Commandment. In addition to such a specific commandment against the bearing of false witness against one's neighbor, three other provisions in Hebrew law helped to make perjury in court a crime no one was likely to take lightly. In the first place, no witness was allowed to stand alone. More than one witness was always called, and no man could be convicted except on the agreeing testimony of at least two witnesses. Furthermore, if it was proved that a witness had testified falsely, the punishment which his untrue testimony was intended to bring upon the accused was imposed upon the false witness himself (Deuteronomy 19:15-21). Finally, the witnesses on whose testimony the accused was convicted were required to act also as the executioners of the sentence (Deuteronomy 17:7). In view of such stringent legal regulations regarding the giving of testimony during a trial, it is not surprising that—except in the rare cases when there was a general breakdown of morality on the part of the civil authorities themselves (I Kings 21:1-13)—perjury in Hebrew court proceedings was practically nonexistent.

Happily, our own courts are also largely free of the kind of perjury against which the Hebrews exercised such an effective control. What decimates the effectiveness of our courts in their effort to maintain order and justice is not so much the giving of perjured testimony by false witnesses as the irresponsible refusal of so many generally decent citizens to give the true testimony which is necessary to convict and restrain the lawbreakers who prey on the persons and properties of their innocent neighbors. Sometimes, as in the case of "bootlegging"—both during and since prohibition days—and illegal gambling, the testimony needed to convict the criminal is withheld by the otherwise innocent citizen because he wishes to participate in the illegal operation in some way, although he would not consider conducting the enterprise himself, and even though he is obviously one of the victims of the operation. Some refuse to testify against such predators because they fear that some means of retaliation may be used against them by those whose interests are injured by such testimony. Most people simply do not want to be bothered.

It is not easy for some people to understand that when they refuse to give evidence to convict the offenders in cases of crimes they have seen committed, or know certainly to have been committed, they are as guilty of bearing a false witness as when they actually perjure themselves in court. By their silence they say that there is no criminal activity in their community—at least none that they know about—and thus give a false impression of

the actual situation. The Ninth Commandment does not *say* that
a person should bear a true witness when it is possible and needed
to control crime and restrain the criminal offender, but the
implication to that effect is clear. Where right and justice are
concerned, it is as much the duty of every citizen to be articulate
in bearing a true witness to and for all his neighbors as it is that
he refrain from bearing a false witness against any one of them.

A form of false witness which is very much like perjury is
slander. While slander is not usually considered by law to be as
serious a crime as perjury, it can be an equally deadly weapon in
the hands of the false witness. Slander is much more widespread
and much more difficult to control than perjury. Perjury can
be easily and clearly defined. Laws against perjury can be formu-
lated and effectively enforced. Slander is a more elusive thing.
It is not confined to the court room. It shuns the open atmosphere
of a legal trial. It is whispered in the corridors and allowed to flow
freely with the current of irresponsible gossip. Slander convicts,
sentences, and punishes its victims in the fickle court of public
opinion. Slander never appears as a definite statement or a direct
charge. It is disseminated and seeps into people's consciousness as
subtle implications and innocent-sounding innuendoes.

While the slander passed across the back fence by means of
old-fashioned person-to-person gossip is still a serious form of false
witness, the danger of this kind of character assassination has
greatly increased with the advent of our modern means of mass
communication. The washroom operator of a few generations ago
who had to buttonhole individually every prospective carrier of
his slanderous inventions has been replaced in these times by
the unprincipled communications expert who knows how to drop
a hint to a newspaper reporter or hand a tip to a television news-
caster precisely worded to give a devastatingly false impression
without quite running afoul of any enforceable libel law. The
use of such lethal slander techniques is unfortunately not always
confined to the individual of deliberate ill-will or the self-
appointed committees of bigotry and misguided partiotism. Because of the almost unbelievably rapid and thorough dissemination of news today, well-meaning and otherwise quite responsible

individuals and groups—even government agencies—through carelessness or indiscretion, may become the unwitting and unwilling architects of widely proclaimed statements and impressions which are quite false and quite damaging to individuals and even whole categories of people.

A great part of the responsibility for preventing the spread of these and other kinds of untruths lies with the newspapers and other news media themselves. While there is generally a high degree of integrity to be found on the part of those who are responsible for the information which reaches us by way of our major news media, there are spots in their performance which leave much to be desired.[12] Irresponsibility in the dissemination of information to the public may be observed in the common practice of "slanting," or "coloring," news stories. Slanting, or coloration, is accomplished by selecting unrepresentative aspects of a news event and presenting them in a way designed to give the impression that they are representative. When such coloring of the news occurs, it is usually done to serve some special interest to which the newspaper or other news agency is officially committed.[13] Certainly, no one would seek to deny to a newspaper or other news agency the right to have and champion certain special interests. These are private institutions, and they are entitled to the rights and privileges enjoyed by other private institutions. It is surely permissible for a newspaper or broadcasting company to hold and proclaim its own private opinion on any subject. This is the purpose and the function of the editorial. But the expression of private opinions should not be confused with newsreporting. To inject private opinion into a news story in a way that distorts the facts and gives an impression that is not true is to bear a false witness and—in the case of a newspaper or other mass communications medium—to betray a public trust.[14]

Reporting a part of a story, however faithfully, which gives a false impression because the rest of the story is not told is also an irresponsible handling of the news. One cannot be excused for such reporting on the ground that he did not have the whole story. It is his business to *get* the whole story before reporting it, if the part he has in hand cannot be reported without creating a false impression.[15] This is indeed the policy which one newspaper has adopted and proposes to follow:

> WE BELIEVE: That it is our duty to KNOW the difference between TRUTH and PROPAGANDA and to use all the strength of our INTELLECT and our INTEGRITY to damn propaganda by refusing to give it space in the columns of our newspapers.
>
> WE BELIEVE: That pure, unadulterated TRUTH is the heartbeat of a FREE PEOPLE and that it is our duty to dig until we are SURE we have the WHOLE TRUTH before we say anything at all.[16]

Adherence to some such standard of principles and procedures would seem to be the obligation of every person engaged in the business of reporting the news as public information, particularly those who make use of any one of our fabulously influential mass communications media.

A form of lying which constitutes a particularly dangerous threat to the stability of society is the commercialized deceit that appears in false advertising. While much of the exaggeration contained in many advertisments is actually more comical than deceptive, and may be understood as a friendly form of rivalry among quite congenial competitors rather than a malicious effort to deceive the public, it is difficult to disprove the validity of Shaw's assertion that "the residue of downright impudent venal lying is enormous."[17] The opinion formed by many responsible observers of advertising techniques in our own country tends to agree with the conclusion reached by Shaw. One appraisal of the industry as it now operates declares that "advertising cares nothing for virtue or love; it prefers, if anything, that man do not develop his reason too much; and as for the classical virtues of the producer, it earnestly hopes these will be forgotten."[18] Fortunately, this is not true of all advertising; but the proportion of advertising of which this is an all too accurate picture is much too great to be ignored.

While it seems fairly certain that the advertising industry itself must bear a great part of the blame for the deception which appears in the presentation of goods and services to the buying public,[19] there is hardly a one of us who is not in some way responsible for this unwholesome situation. Certainly the operators of the mass communications media which carry false advertising claims and deceptively presented commercial programs must accept a part of the responsibility.[20] A large and basic share of the responsibility has to be borne by the marketers themselves who, operating in an economy of abundance, cannot resist the temptation to make an irresponsible use of desire-creating advertisement as a means of stimulating sales and expanding their businesses.[21] The individual is also partly responsible for the general breakdown of moral sensitivity which makes false advertising on any scale of dangerously large proportions possible. Public deceit is nothing more than a composite reflection of personal dishonesty. Public morality can never rise higher than personal integrity. The effectiveness of false advertising on the part of marketers is dependent upon the individual's willingness and desire to get something for nothing.[22]

It is not necessary to carry the examination of modern forms of lying any further in order to appreciate the seriousness of the problem which the practice of bearing false witness poses for our generation. Even such a brief survey of the situation as this makes it abundantly clear that Albert Rasmussen was right when, speaking of the moral climate of our times, he said that "honesty needs a new look."[23] To restore honesty to its rightful place of sovereignty as the principle by which all our dealings with one another are ordered is one of the most urgent needs of our generation. The actual enthronement of truth in human relations is not an easy accomplishment, but it is essential to the stability of society and the progress of the race.

In the up-hill fight against false witness and the personal and social corruption which it breeds we can be encouraged by the fact that our efforts are aided by the basic truth-character of being itself. Carlyle was not being merely rhetorical when he said that "if you know the truth and do it, the Universe itself seconds you, bears you on to sure victory everywhere: and, observe, to sure defeat everywhere if you do *not* the truth."[24] Every exercise of integrity, even on the part of the least individual, summons to his side a fateful force inherent in the nature of being itself—a force which Boris Pasternak has called "the irresistible power of unarmed truth."[25] Sometimes what is needed most is simply to get the truth said. We betray the truth more often by craven silence than by spoken lies. James Russell Lowell was being practical as well as poetic when he said:

> Get but the truth once uttered, and 'tis like
> A star new-born, that drops into its place,
> And which, once circling in its placid round,
> Not all the tumult of the earth can shake.[26]

It was practical advice also—and advice quite relevant to our situation—which the author of Ephesians gave when he said to his readers: "Therefore, putting away falsehood, let every one speak the truth with his neighbor, *for we are members one of another*" (Ephesians 4:25, italics mine).

X

THE DISCIPLINE
OF DESIRE

There is a new science in process of development which could make the Tenth Commandment obsolete. It is called "biocontrol." Biocontrol is the manipulation of mental processes, emotional reactions, appetites, and sense perceptions by means of bioelectrical signals which are brought to bear on the central nervous system of the subject under control. The absolute control of a country's entire population has been envisioned as one possibility of this science. All that would be necessary to effect such a control, as explained by one authority,[1] is that each child be equipped shortly after birth with a socket mounted under the scalp and having electrodes in contact with selected areas of brain tissue. Later, a miniature radio receiver could be plugged into this socket. Thereafter, the subject's impulses and activities could be completely controlled by bioelectric signals emanating from state-operated transmitters.

Such a use of biocontrol, or any other equally efficient system of external control over human thought and action, would indeed make the Tenth Commandment—and every other moral principle —obsolete. The only trouble with this kind of control is that it would also make the human race obsolete. Man's humanity consists essentially in his possession and use of the ability to think, feel, evaluate, choose, decide, and act for himself. As soon as any person allows these normal human functions to be taken over and manipulated by any external system of control, he ceases to be a human being and becomes a mere biochemical robot. The

Tenth Commandment has nothing to say to a robot—of any kind. It is designed to keep men aware of the fact that their existence and fulfillment as human beings depend upon a voluntary control and direction of their own thoughts, feelings, desires, and actions, and to encourage them to exercise such self-control in all their experiences.

THE NATURE OF DESIRE

Like the science of biocontrol, the Tenth Commandment is concerned about that area of mans' being where will, thoughts, feelings, appetites, passions, desires, emotions, and inner urges exist and exert their influence. The exact nature and seat of these human faculties and functions has never been perfectly or positively determined. One explanation occasionally suggested in biblical thought is that the passions which determine man's attitudes and actions on particular occasions are due to the visitation of a good or evil spirit. This idea is contained in the account of King Saul's erratic behavior (I Samuel 10:9-11; 11:6; 18:10-11; 19:8-11, 23-24), the story of the mad Gadarenes (Matthew 8:28-33), and the record of the defection of Judas.[4] According to a more mature and consistent biblical view, the various and frequently conflicting passions which are the motivating forces behind all human actions are seen in their basic character as a part of the inner nature of man's own being. This concept of the motivating forces in human experience is expressed in the Old Testament proverb which says of man that "as he thinketh in his heart, so is he" (Proverbs 23:7, K.J.V.); in Jesus' statement that "out of the heart come evil thoughts, murder, adultery, fornication, theft, false witness, slander" (Matthew 15:19); and in the confession of Paul who said of his own contrary emotions: "I delight in the law of God, in my inmost self, but I see in my members another law at war with the law of my mind and making me captive to the law of sin *which dwells in my members*" (Romans 7:22-23, italics mine).

The latter view is the one most strongly supported by the findings and conclusions of modern study. That human beings have a certain number of natural drives, or compelling desires, which are among the motivating forces that help to determine their attitudes and actions, is a fact which has been discovered by scientific research as well as spiritual insight. Some of man's more elemental urges, such as the drive to procure food when he is hungry, the inclination to avoid physical pain, and the compulsion toward procreation of his own kind, are mainly physiological in character. Many human drives, however, have little if any physical basis. They are urges toward ego satisfaction, rather than physical satisfaction. Among these are the tendency to dominate, the wish to belong, the craving for social recognition and approval, the longing for happiness, and the desire for security.

The normal cycle of events which one experiences in connection with the motivating influence of such a drive is the building up of tension as a result of the urge toward satisfaction, the gratification of the desire, and the subsequent subsiding of tension experienced as a tranquil and somewhat triumphant feeling of general well-being. Human desire, however, does not always run this normal course. Desire frequently comes into conflict with environmental conditions which limit gratification, postpone it, or prohibit it altogether. The desires of one person often come into conflict with the desires of another person in such a way that those of one or the other cannot be gratified, or in such a way that some or all of the desires of both are partially or totally frustrated. There is also nearly always within the individual himself a more or less serious conflict among the various drives which are the motivating forces in his experience. Even when man's desires do not come into conflict with one another and are not frustrated by the limitations of environment, they may take an unnatural direction or run to an excess which may constitute a serious problem both for the individual concerned and for the society in which he lives.[2]

Casual consideration of these facts about the fundamental drives which help to determine man's attitudes and actions may easily lead one to the conclusion that human desire itself is a bad thing and should—if possible—be eliminated. This is indeed the very conclusion which has been reached and accepted within some quite respectable systems of thought. The Buddhists, for example, believe that man is able to find peace and experience the fulfillment of his being only if he annihilates all his desires and thus enters a state of complete passionlessness.[3] In Buddhist dogmatics "Nirvana" is defined literally as a "blowing out," that is, the blowing out or extinction of the fires of passion in the one who attains to full release from the compelling influences of desire.[4] Other traditions, including both Hebrew and Christian thought, accept the fundamental drives of the human person as a potentially beneficial part of the nature of man which contribute to the fulfillment of his being when they function normally. Human desire is considered evil only when it is perverted or when it runs to excess. This understanding of the fundamental nature of desire is evident in the Old Testament teaching which declares that "the desire of the righteous ends only in good" (Proverbs 11:23). This idea was expressed also by Jesus when—commenting on some of the basic wants of his contemporaries—he said: "But seek first his kingdom and his righteousness, and all these things shall be yours as well" (Matthew 6:33).

Recognizing the conflict caused by human passions, Alexander Pope raised a serious question as to whether it might not be better if man were without such passions, then gave an answer favoring the situation as it is.

> Better for us, perhaps, it might appear,
> Were there all harmony, all virtue here;
> That never air or ocean felt the wind;
> That never passion discomposed the mind.
> But all subsists by elemental strife;
> And passions are the elements of life.
> The gen'ral order, since the whole began,
> Is kept in nature, and is kept in man.[5]

Modern psychology begins with a similar acceptance of human passion as not being bad in itself, but as capable of enriching or destroying life, depending upon whether the flow of passion in human experience is normal, or perverted and excessive. James

McCosh, for example, saw in human passions—or emotions—"the main means of our happiness or our misery. They are not to be eradicated," he stoutly maintained, "but guided."[6]

THE EXERCISE OF SELF-CONTROL

This is the point at which any realistic effort to understand and obey the Tenth Commandment must begin. The Tenth Commandment forbids covetousness; but the prohibition against covetousness is qualified by a specific statement concerning the things coveted and the conditions under which they are coveted, which makes it quite clear that what the Commandment forbids is not the experience of desire itself, but the unbridled and irresponsible grasping of desire which debases one's own character and injures his neighbor. The term "covetousness" came into the English language by way of the Old French word *cuveitier*, from the Latin *cupere*, which means "to desire." Some form of the word "covet" is used to translate three different Hebrew words in the Old Testament, which mean respectively, to delight in, to wish for, and to plunder. In the New Testament "covet," or "covetousness," is used to translate five different Greek words, which mean respectively, to long for, to have warmth of feeling for or against, to reach out after, to be fond of silver, and to be avaricious.[7] Thus while Jesus could properly warn those whom he taught to "beware of all covetousness" (Luke 12:15), Paul could encourage the Corinthians with equal propriety to "covet earnestly the best gifts" (I Corinthians 12:31, K.J.V.). This overloading of some of our English words with many meanings, some of which are quite opposite, makes it necessary for us to examine carefully the sense in which any one of these words is used before we settle on the meaning of the statement in which it appears.

Basically, to covet is to desire; and we have seen that the possession and exercise of the ability to feel, think, desire, choose, will, and act for one's self is of the nature of, and essential to, the existence of man as a human being. We cannot, therefore, understand the Tenth Commandment as a prohibition against the experience of desire. We should understand it rather as a prohibition against the experience of desire which runs rampant over reason and the rights of others. It is not wrong for a man to covet (desire) a house, or a wife, or a servant, or a work animal; but it is wrong for him to covet his *neighbor's* house, or wife, or servant, or work animal, because there is in the desire for *that which belongs to another* the seed of a willingness to deprive him of it unjustly, a seed which may grow all too readily into the act itself. This is the sense in which the word "covet" is used in the Tenth Commandment. The covetousness which the Tenth Commandment forbids is a covetousness which must be understood as a willingness and a wish to injure one's neighbor in order to gratify one's own desire. And since the gratification of desire on these terms injures and ultimately destroys the one who indulges in it, the covetousness which the Tenth Commandment forbids must be understood too as a suicidal willingness and wish to destroy one's own self also.

Desire is not a bad thing in itself. Basically and potentially, desire is a good thing, because, as Thomas Aquinas has reminded us, "since all things flow from the Divine Will, all things in their own way are inclined towards good of their own natural tendency."[8] Desire, however, like everything else that is distinctively human, can be perverted and made to serve as an instrument of evil. In its actual expression as a motivating force in human experience, desire is good or bad depending upon the character of the object desired, the circumstances under which it is desired, and the degree to which it is desired. Desire is bad when the thing desired is bad. Desire for even a good thing is bad when the desire is one which can be gratified only by unjustly depriving another person of something which rightfully belongs to him or by injuring him in some other way. Desire for even a good thing is bad also when the intensity with which it is experienced is so great that it constitutes an actual injury to the one who feels it, or leads him to injure someone else, or when it is felt with an intensity sufficient to constitute a threat of injury to the one who experiences it, or to someone else. Desire is good when the object desired is good, when it is desired in proper moderation, and when the experience of the desire or its gratification does not constitute or lead to an injury or a threat of injury to the self or to anyone else.

In his book, *Desire and the Universe*,[9] John K. Shryock sees the problem of desire as having two major aspects. One part of the problem has to do with the question of what sort of creature a man really ought to be. Most people want to experience the fullest possible realization of their potentialities as human beings, but what, precisely, is a perfect man supposed to be like? What are the things he should desire as the fulfillment of his nature and destiny? The second aspect of the problem is posed by the limitations which environment imposes upon the realization of our desires. There are two courses we can follow in the attempt to prevent or at least lessen the shock of this collision between our desires and our environment. We can cut the cloth of desire to fit the pattern of environment, or we can try to reshape the character of our environment into something a little more compatible with our desires.

The second of these two methods by which we may attempt to solve the problem of desire is the one which modern man has used more extensively. This is the way of science. The method science uses in its approach to the problem of desire is to attempt to change man's environment so that it will permit and contribute to the gratification of his desires. To this end and with this effect science has radically changed the character of our environment. Much if not all of this change may be viewed as being—in the long run—an improvement. Science has provided many of the things we wish for, some of them in almost unbelievable abundance. But science has not solved the problem of desire. Science has given us many of the things we want, but science has made no progress toward closing the gap of unfulfilled desire. Science has sharpened the edge of desire, but science has not brought to desire either direction or discipline. The growth of our scientifically stepped-up industrial production has not even kept pace with the growth of our desires. Modern science has only proved what Aristotle declared to be true many centuries ago: "it is of the nature of desire not to be satisfied."[10]

Not only has science not been able to control or keep pace

with the growing demands of man's insatiable appetites in the commercialized expression of its genius, but it has actually done more than anything else to stimulate these inordinate desires. Our scientifically equipped and operated business enterprises work as hard as they can to produce the commodities needed to supply human wants, and at the same time spend billions of dollars annually for advertising in a deliberate and frantic effort to create new and greater wants. These two aspects of contemporary business enterprise are apparently considered by most manufacturers and merchants to be equally proper and equally essential to the successful and appropriate functioning of the modern economic process. Perhaps they are, at least to some extent. Certainly the stimulation of desire is not necessarily all bad. The awakening of old desires and the creation of new desires are among the things that are essential to any progress of the human race toward those ends for which it was created. But the way modern business works at the job of supplying our wants on the one hand, and stimulating our desires on the other, with no apparent understanding of or concern for the effects which the total process might have on the moral character of individuals and society, seems to create certain frustrating contradictions within the economy itself. It is not unusual, for example, to hear manufacturers protesting that the wages demanded by their employees are exorbitant to the point of constituting a serious threat to the survival of the business itself, without giving any indication that they are aware of the fact that their employees are asking for these exorbitant wages so that they can buy the commodities which the manufacturers are producing and offering for sale and thereby satisfy a desire which was stimulated in the first place wholly or partly by the billion dollar advertisements promoted and paid for by the manufacturers themselves. While thus running itself to death on the treadmill of human desire, modern business has raised the material standard of living to an all-time high, but in doing so it has also lifted the level of discontent to the point of moral bankruptcy.

Nothing we have said by way of analyzing the dilemma of modern business should be understood as an effort to place all the blame for the current perversions and excesses of desire at the door of today's economic enterprise. Perhaps business is the one institution in our society which should be blamed least for the running away of our desires. We have seen that we cannot solve the problem of desire by eliminating desire, because desire is a necessary part of the being of man which cannot be eliminated without eliminating man himself. Trying to solve the problem of desire by eliminating desire—even if that were possible—would be like cutting off our feet to solve the problem of shoes. We have seen also that it is never possible for production to catch up with desire, for the attainment of the object of desire always gives birth to a greater desire. The solution to the problem of desire lies not in the elimination of all desire, or in the satisfaction of all desire, but in the discipline of desire. Desire is not to be eliminated or overindulged, but controlled and directed. Business cannot be expected to contribute a great deal to the control and direction of desire. The main responsibility of business is to provide the goods and services which are needed to satisfy a large part of man's legitimate desires. The control of desire is mainly the responsibility of other social institutions, particularly the home, the school, the church, and the state. Business can be blamed for needlessly and irresponsibly overstimulating desire in many instances. Business can also be expected to assume its fair share of responsibility for helping to develop morally and socially acceptable desires and for helping to supply meaningful satisfactions for these desires. For business to bear this responsibility, however, it must be led by men whose own desires have been properly disciplined long before they have reached the age required for responsible participation in the economic process. Such early discipline of desire must be provided for the most part by processes other than the economic one.

No institution bears more of the responsibility for the discipline of desire than the home. Desire takes its shape and receives its bent early, while the child is still mostly under parental care and guidance. If the parents fail at this point, what the school and the church and the state can and ought to do by way of helping the individual achieve a mature and responsible experience of desire

is limited and made extremely difficult. Sir Roger L'Estrange was
more right than we usually realize when he said that:

> All the public outrages of a destroying tyranny and op-
> pression, are but childish appetites let alone until they are
> grown ungovernable. . . . We have the seeds of virtue in us,
> as well as of vice; and whenever we take a strong bias, tis
> not out of a moral incapacity to do better, but for want
> of a careful manage and discipline, to set us right at first.
> . . . It is with our passions, as it is with fire and water, they
> are good servants, but bad masters.[11]

It is the first duty of all those who participate in the rearing and
the education of children—particularly their parents—to guide
them in the discipline of their desires so that they may become
good servants to them, and not bad masters. Children should be
provided in the home from their earliest years with good music,
good pictures, good books, proper ideals, moral principles, religious instruction, a natural experience of worship, gentle but
firm direction and discipline in the formation and exercise of
good habits, wholesome attitudes, and satisfying ways of expressing themselves; for this is the time when an individual's desires are
largely shaped, and these are the things which determine to a great
extent the character and expression of the desires which he will
experience for the rest of his life.

The end of all the instruction and guidance which may be
given to the child in the discipline of desire should be the achieve-
ment of self-discipline on the part of the individual himself. By
their very nature the desires which an individual experiences are
so personal and so inward that they can never be controlled by
anyone or anything except the will and intelligence of the person
himself. This fact needs urgently to be brought to bear on our
current concern for liberty. If we do not wish to be controlled
arbitrarily by some force from beyond ourselves, we must be
willing and able to control ourselves, and basically this means
that we must be willing and able to discipline our own desires.
No one has made this fact clearer than Edmund Burke did almost
two hundred years ago when he wrote:

A TRANSFER FROM THE PARENT TO THE CHILD THE DISCIPLINING POWER

> Men are qualified for civil liberty in exact proportion to their disposition to put chains upon their own appetites—in proportion as their love of justice is above their rapacity, —in proportion as their soundness and sobriety of understanding is above their vanity and presumption,—in proportion as they are more disposed to listen to the counsels of the wise and good, in preference to the flattery of knaves. Society cannot exist unless a controlling power upon will and appetite is placed somewhere; and the less of it there is within, the more there must be without. It is ordained in the eternal constitution of things, that men of intemperate minds cannot be free. Their passions forge their fetters.[12]

The Tenth Commandment cannot curb a person's covetousness, or any one of his other desires. It was not intended to provide such compulsion. It was intended to remind every man that he is responsible for the direction and discipline of his own desires. Man is the kind of creature who *can* direct and discipline all his desires in keeping with the nature of his being and in a way which makes possible the realization of all his potentialities as a child of God. But man is not the kind of creature who *must* exercise such a control over his desires. Man is the kind of creature who can and sometimes does let his desires run to excess, and be perverted. Man is the kind of creature who can destroy himself by choosing *not* to discipline himself. This capacity of man to choose fulfillment or destruction for his own life is what we mean by human freedom.

While man is *free* he is not *alone* in the working out of his eternal destiny. The God who made him in the beginning continues to nurture him in the course of his adventures with good and evil. With fatherly concern God struggles along with man in his obedience and his rebellion. God does not take away man's freedom to determine the nature of his own response, but he does speak to man authoritatively, persuasively, and persistently. God speaks to man in the requirements of the law, in the judgments and the pleadings of the prophets, and in the Person of his Son, Jesus Christ. In Jesus Christ the sovereignty of God is manifested and the salvation of man is accomplished, not by the compulsions of force but by the persuasions of love. In Jesus Christ, God wins man's devotion and obedience, not by making his will irresistible but by making himself available. The discipline of desire is possible because God has made his grace available in the Person of Christ. When we accept this grace "the love of Christ controls us" (II Corinthians 5:14).

NOTES AND ACKNOWLEDGEMENTS

THE PRIORITY OF GOD

1. James Thomson, "Spring," *The Seasons*, The Poetical Works of James Thomson, Vol. II, p. 38, lines 851-852. Boston: Houghton Mifflin & Company, n.d.
2. John Dryden and Mr. Lee, *Oedipus*. Edinburgh: J. Robertson, 1774, Act IV, p. 69.
3. *The Philadelphia Tribune*, May 3, 1960, pp. 1, 9.

THE WORSHIP OF GOD

1. Walter Rauschenbusch, *A Theology for the Social Gospel*, p. 49. New York: The Macmillian Company, 1917. (Paperback reprint by Abingdon Press, 1961.)
2. Elton Trueblood, *Foundations for Reconstruction*, p. 22. New York: Harper & Brothers, 1949.
3. A. A. Vasiliev, *History of the Byzantine Empire*, Vol. I, pp. 315-323. University of Wisconsin Studies in the Social Sciences and History, No. 13, Madison, Wisconsin, 1928.
4. Owen M. Weatherly, *The Fulfillment of Life*, pp. 139-149. Richmond, Virginia: John Knox Press, 1959.
5. John Calvin, *Institutes of the Christian Religion*, Translated by Henry Beveridge, p. 439. Grand Rapids, Michigan: William B. Eerdmans Company.
6. Von Ogden Vogt, *The Primacy of Worship*, p. 46. Boston: Starr King Press, 1958.
7. Bernard E. Meland, *Modern Man's Worship*, p. 46. New York: Harper & Brothers, 1934.
8. George Edward Barton, *The Pipe of Desire and Other Plays*, pp. 35-41. The Old Corner Bookstore Inc., D. B. Updike, The Merrymount Press, 1905.

THE INTEGRITY OF MAN

1. Genesis 25:24-25. *A Dictionary of the Bible*, ed. by James Hastings, Vol. I, p. 733. New York: Charles Scribner's Sons, 1901.
2. Richard B. Brandt, "Name," *An Encyclopedia of Religion*, ed. by Vergilius Ferm, p. 516. New York: The Philosophical Society, 1945.
3. Acts 17:28. Quoted by Paul to the Athenians, and believed to be a line from a poem by Epimenides.
4. "Baptist, a Popular Name," *The Baptist World*, June 1960, p. 11.
5. John J. Weaver, Dean, The Cathedral of St. Paul, Detroit, "The Urban Church," an unpublished pamphlet, 1959.

6. Mencius, *The Works of Mencius*, Book IV, Part I, Chapter 12, *The Chinese Classics*, second edition revised, translated by James Legge, Vol. II, p. 303. Oxford: The Clarendon Press, 1895.
7. James Russell Lowell, "Rousseau and the Sentimentalists," *Among My Books*, p. 358. New York: Houghton Mifflin Company, 1898.

THE RHYTHM OF LIFE

1. Herman Wouk, *This Is My God*, p. 60. Garden City, New York: Doubleday & Company, Inc., 1959.
2. Samuel M. Segal, *The Sabbath Book*, p. XIII. New York: Thomas Yoseloff, 1942.
3. Hutton Webster, "Sabbath (Primitive)," *Encyclopedia of Religion and Ethics*, ed. by James Hastings, pp. 885-886. New York: Charles Scribner's Sons, 1908.
4. Theophilus G. Pinches, "Sabbath (Babylonian)," *Ibid.*, pp. 889-890.
5. George Dana Boardman, *The Ten Commandments*, p. 110. Philadelphia: American Baptist Publication Society, 1889.
   R. W. Dale, *The Ten Commandments*, p. 110. New York: George H. Doran Company, no date.
   Frederick W. Robertson, *Sermons Preached at Brighton*, p. 84. New York: Harper & Brothers, no date.
6. A. Purnell Bailey, "Bread of Life," Richmond, Virginia: *Richmond News-Leader*, July 30, 1957, p. 2, column 1.
7. For an up-to-date legal discussion of the question considered in this section the reader is referred to the opinion written by Judge Raymond Pace Alexander in support of his decisions in the cases of Commonwealth vs. Cavelerro and Commonwealth vs. Levenston, Court of Quarter Sessions of Philadelphia County, filed April 20, 1960, in which the Pennsylvania Sunday Law of 1959 was held unconstitutional as in violation of both the Pennsylvania Constitution and the Constitution of the United States.
8. *Ibid.*

THE CONTINUITY OF LIFE

1. Thomas Carlyle, "Characteristics," *The Harvard Classics*, ed. by Charles W. Eliot, p. 367. New York: P. F. Collier & Son, 1909.
2. George Santayana, "The Flux and Constancy in Human Nature," *The Life of Reason*, p. 84. New York: Charles Scribner's Sons, 1953.
3. George G. N. Byron, *Childe Harold's Pilgrimage*, Canto IV, Stanza 108, p. 194. New York: Harper & Brothers, 1945.
4. Alfred North Whitehead, "Past, Present, Future," *Adventures of Ideas*, p. 256. New York: The Macmillan Company, 1933.
5. R. H. Charles, *The Decalogue*, pp. 174-175. London: T & T Clarke, 1923.

THE SACREDNESS OF LIFE

1. *Uniform Crime Reports for the United States*, p. 6. Federal Bureau of Investigation, U.S. Department of Justice, Washington 25, D.C., 1959.
2. *Ibid.*, p. 4.
3. There were 90,604 accidental deaths in the U. S. during 1958. *Statistical Abstract of the United States*, 81st Edition, p. 68. Prepared under the direction of Edwin D. Goldfield, U.S. Department of Commerce, U.S. Printing Office, Washington, D. C., 1960.
4. *Statistical Abstract of the United States, op. cit.*, pp. 65, 564.

5. *Information Please Almanac,* pp. 348, 416. Planned and supervised by Dan Golenpaul Associates. New York: McGraw-Hill, 1960.
6. Information contained in *The Luckless Legion,* a booklet published by the Travelers Insurance Companies, as quoted in *Missions,* an International Baptist Magazine, vol. 157, no. 6, June 1959, p. 14.
7. *Statistical Abstract of the United States, op. cit.,* pp. 65, 141. The number of suicides reported for 1959 was 18,330. However, this figure does not include those in Alaska, Hawaii, or the country's armed forces. For some years the total has been reported to be as high as 22,000 (Karl Menninger, *Man Against Himself,* p. 38. New York: Harcourt, Brace and Company, 1938).
8. Karl A. Menninger, *Man Against Himself,* p. 470. New York: Harcourt, Brace and Company, 1938. Used by permission.
9. *Ibid.*
10. Hugo Adam Bedau, "The Death Penalty Today," *The Christian Century,* March 18, 1959, p. 32.
11. *Uniform Crime Reports for the United States, op. cit.,* p. 14.
12. Bedau, *op. cit.,* p. 32.
13. *The World Almanac and Fact Book,* ed. by Harry Hansen, p. 742. New York: New York World-Telegram, 1960.
14. Niccolo Machiavelli, *The Prince and The Discourses,* p. 53. Translated by Luigi Ricci, revised by E. R. P. Vincent. New York: The Modern Library, 1940.
15. Lloyd Lewis, *Sherman, Fighting Prophet,* p. 636. New York: Harcourt, Brace and Company, 1932.
16. Smedley D. Butler, *War Is a Racket,* p. 52. New York: Round Table Press, Inc., 1935.

THE DIGNITY OF PERSONALITY

1. Ernest W. Burgess and Harvey Locke, *The Family,* pp. 212-213. New York: American Book Company, 1945.
2. Read Bain, "Producing Marriageable Personalities," *Family, Marriage and Parenthood,* Second Edition, ed. by Howard Becker and Reuben Hill, p. 192. Boston: D. C. Heath and Company, 1955.
3. Don Martindale, "The Variety of the Human Family," *Ibid.,* p. 150.
4. Boardman, *The Ten Commandments,* pp. 211, 220.
5. Conrad Henry Moehlman, *The Story of the Ten Commandments,* p. 202. New York: Harcourt, Brace and Company, 1928.
6. Mabel A. Elliott, "The Scope and Meaning of Divorce," *Family, Marriage and Parenthood, op. cit.,* pp. 693-694.
7. *Ibid.,* pp. 693, 704-705.
8. Robert S. W. Pollard, *The Problem of Divorce,* p. 2. London: C. A. Watts & Co., Ltd., 1958.

THE RESPONSIBILITY OF STEWARDSHIP

1. Arthur Twining Hadley, *Freedom and Responsibility,* p. 159. New York: Charles Scribner's Sons, 1903.
2. Charles Lincoln Taylor, Jr., "Old Testament Foundations," *Christianity and Property,* p. 12. Philadelphia: The Westminster Press, 1947.
3. Vernon Bartlett, "The Biblical and Early Christian Idea of Property," *Property: Its Duties and Rights,* p. 88. London: Macmillan and Company, 1913.
4. Richard Stanley Merrill Emrick, "New Testament Teaching," *Christianity and Property, op. cit.,* p. 36.

5. *Crime in the United States*, pp. 3, 75. Uniform Crime Reports—1959, Washington, D. C.: Federal Bureau of Investigation, U.S. Department of Justice, September 1960.
6. "Public Gets Trimmed By Drug Ads, Unit Says," News report of Congressional investigating committee findings published in the *Richmond Times-Dispatch*, Richmond, Virginia, August 11, 1958, p. 6.
"Toothpaste Ads, FEC Draw Fire," News report of Congressional investigating committee findings published in the *Richmond Times-Dispatch*, Richmond, Virginia, August 18, 1958, p. 6.
7. *Alcohol Education*, p. 34. Washington, D. C.: National Temperance League, Third Quarter, 1960.
Report, Chicago: American Business Men's Research Foundation, 1958-1959 Annual, Vol. XVI, No. 6, p. 41.
Christianity Today, Washington, D. C.: Christianity Today, Inc., Vol. V, No. 4, p. 27.
8. "Gambling," ed. by Morris Plascome and Edwin J. Lucas, *The Annals of the American Academy of Political and Social Science*, Philadelphia: The American Academy of Political and Social Science, May 1950, Vol. 269, p. VII.
Alson J. Smith, "The Churches and Gambling," *The Christian Century*, Chicago: The Christian Century Foundation, April 29, 1959, Vol. 76, No. 1, p. 512.
Clyde Brion Davis, *Something for Nothing*, pp. 16-18. J. P. Lippincott Company, 1956.
9. Calvin, *Institutes of the Christian Religion*, p. 476.
10. Louis O. Kelson and Mortimer J. Adler, "The Concealment of the Declining Productivity of Labor in Our Present Economy," *The Capitalist Manifesto*, pp. 256-265. New York: Random House, 1958.
"And Then There's Featherbedding," Editorial, *Life*, p. 30. Chicago: Time, Inc., June 1, 1959.
11. Martin Luther, "On Trading and Usury," translated by C. M. Jacobs, *Works of Martin Luther*, p. 16. Philadelphia: A. J. Holman Company and the Castle Press, 1931.
12. C. B. Deane, former U.S. Congressman, as quoted in an editorial in *The Christian Index*, p. 6. Atlanta: Baptist Convention of the State of Georgia, March 17, 1960.
13. C. Harry Kahn, of the National Bureau of Economic Research at Rutgers University, as reported in an editorial in the *Philadelphia Inquirer*, p. 22. December 10, 1959.

THE SANCTITY OF TRUTH

1. Cf above, pp. 84 and 100-102.
2. Washington Gladden, "Ultima Veritas," *Masterpieces of Religious Verse*, ed. by James Dalton Morrison, p. 383. New York: Harper & Brothers, 1948.
3. Edgar Sheffield Brightman, "Platonism," *Encyclopedia of Religion*, ed. by Vergilius Ferm, p. 594. New York: The Philosophical Library, 1945.
Ernst Cassirer, "Truth," *Encyclopaedia Britannica*, ed. by Walter Yust, Vol. 22, p. 522. Chicago: Encyclopaedia Britannica, Inc., 1947.
Plato, *The Republic*, *The Dialogues of Plato*, translated by B. Jowett, Third Edition, Vol. III, pp. 173-213. Oxford University Press, London: Humphey Milford, 1892.
4. Ancient Egyptian "Hymn," *The Dwellers on the Nile*, translated by E. A. Wallace Budge, Second Edition, p. 131. London: The Religious Tract Society, 1891.

5. Psalm 119:142. *The Bible, An American Translation*, translated by J. M. Powis Smith, p. 569. Chicago: The University of Chicago Press, 1935. Italics mine.

6. Whitehead, *Adventures of Ideas*, pp. 269-270.

7. Russell W. Davenport, *The Dignity of Man*, pp. 269-270. New York: Harper & Brothers, 1950.

8. James H. Thornwell, *Discourse on Truth*, pp. 157-158. New York: Robert Carter and Brothers, 1869.

9. Ralph Waldo Emerson, "Prudence," *Essays*, First Series, *The Complete Works of Ralph Waldo Emerson*, Vol. II, p. 237. Concord Edition, New York: Houghton Mifflin and Company, 1904.

10. Mark Twain, Following the Equator, *The Writings of Mark Twain*, Hillcrest Edition, Vol. VI, p. 224. Hartford: The American Publishing Company, 1908.

11. Joshua 7:1-26. Cf. Frank G. Slaughter, *The Scarlet Cord*, pp. 295-303. Garden City, New York: Doubleday & Company, Inc., 1956.

12. James Batal *et al.*, *Your Newspaper*, pp. VII, 13, 51, 88-89. New York: The Macmillan Company, 1947.

13. Emory S. Bogardus, *The Making of Public Opinion*, p. 48. New York: Association Press, 1951.

14. Batal *et al., op. cit.*, p. 69.

15. Harry Scherf, *Truths, Half-Truths and Bunk in American Civilization*, pp. 13-14, 82, 143. New York: Exposition Press, 1952.

16. *Richmond Home News*, Vol. I, No. 1, p. 1. Richmond, Virginia, October 16, 1958.

17. George Bernard Shaw, *Everybody's Political What's What?*, p. 295. New York: Dodd, Mead and Company, 1944.

18. Ralph B. Thompson, "Christian Virtues in an Age of Abundance," Chicago: *The Christian Century*, The Christian Century Foundation, Vol. 74, No. 51, p. 1509. December 18, 1957.

19. "Industry Primer Shows Why It's Hard to Set Responsibility," *Life*, Chicago: Time, Inc., Vol. 47, No. 20, p. 32. November 16, 1959.

20. Richard N. Goodwin, "Committee Investigator Reveals How Fixers Seduced Innocents," *Life*, Chicago: Time, Inc., Vol. 47, No. 20, pp. 30-31. November 16, 1959.

21. Thompson, *op. cit.*, pp. 1508-1510.

22. Joseph H. Appel, "Introduction," *The Fight for Truth in Advertising*, by H. J. Kenner, pp. xiii-xiv. New York: Round Table Press, Inc., 1936.

23. Albert Terrill Rasmussen, *Christian Social Ethics*, p. 47. Englewood Cliffs, New Jersey: Prentice-Hall, Inc., 1956.

24. Thomas Carlyle, "Stump-Orator," Latter-Day Pamphlets, No. V, *The Works of Thomas Carlyle*, Centenary Edition, Vol. 20, p. 180. London: Chapman and Hall, Limited, 1907.

25. Boris Pasternak, *Dr. Zhivago*, p. 42. New York: Pantheon Books, Inc., 1958.

26. James Russell Lowell, "A Glance Behind the Curtain," *The Complete Poetical Works of James Russell Lowell*, Cambridge Edition, p. 51. New York: Houghton, Mifflin and Company, 1896.

THE DISCIPLINE OF DESIRE

1. Curtiss R. Schafer, as quoted in "Biocontrol," *Time*, New York: Time, Inc., Vol. LXVII, No. 16, pp. 74-75. October 15, 1956.

2. Luella Cole, *Psychology of Adolescence*, revised edition, pp. 81-87. New York: Rinehart and Company, Inc., 1942.

3. "The Brahmana," From *The Dhammapada*, ascribed to Buddha himself,

Man and Spirit: The Speculative Philosophers, ed. by Saxe Commins and Robert N. Linscott, pp. 164-167. New York: Random House, 1947.

4. *Encyclopaedia Britannica,* Vol. 16, p. 464.

5. Alexander Pope, *An Essay on Man,* lines 165-172, *The Works of Alexander Pope, Esq.,* Vol. III, pp. 58-60. London: C. Bathurst, *et al.,* 1770.

6. James McCosh, *Psychology, The Motive Powers,* p. 192. New York: Charles Scribner's Sons, 1894.

7. Andrew K. Rule, "Convetousness," *Twentieth Century Encyclopedia of Religious Knowledge,* p. 307. Grand Rapids: Baker Book House, 1955.

8. Thomas Aquinas, *The Summa Theologica of Thomas Aquinas,* Part I, Question 59, First Article, translated by Fathers of the English Dominican Province, p. 380. London: R&T Washbourne, Ltd., Second Number, 1912.

9. John K. Shryock, *Desire and the Universe,* pp. 13-15. Philadelphia: The Centaur Press, 1935.

10. Aristotle, *The Politics of Aristotle,* Book II, translated by Benjamin Jowett, p. 37. Oxford: The Clarendon Press, 1885.

11. Sir Roger L'Estrange, *Fables of Aesop,* Eighth Edition Corrected, pp. 47-48. London: A. Bettesworth, *et al.,* 1738.

12. Edmund Burke, "Letter to a Member of the National Assembly," *The Writings and Speeches of Edmund Burke,* pp. 51-52. Boston: Little, Brown and Company, 1901.